The whole BIBLE in a year for MIDDLE SCHOOL

50 LESSONS
FROM GENESIS TO REVELATION!

The whole BIBLE in a year for MIDDLE SCHOOL

50 LESSONS
FROM GENESIS TO REVELATION!

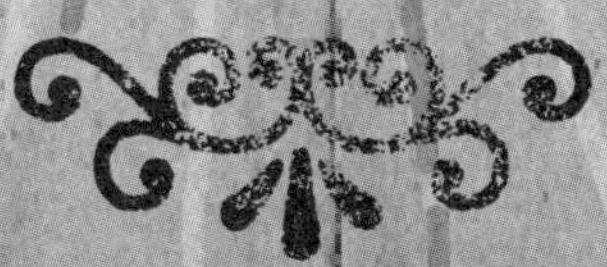

HOWARD ANDRUEJOL

VALERIA LEYS

e625.com

e625.com

The whole Bible in a year for Middle School
Howard Andruejol, Valeria Leys
Originally published in Spanish
Published by e625® © 2024
Dallas, Texas
United States of America

ISBN: 978-1-954149-52-6

Translated by: David Ortíz
Edited by: Sarah Huge
Designed by: Creatorstudio.net

TABLE OF CONTENTS

"All Scripture is inspired by God and is profitable."

2 Timothy 3:16 (CSB)

We are very happy to bring you this series of lessons from the whole Bible. This series will take you on a fascinating tour of a library that consists of sixty-six volumes, which will allow you to get to know God's character, His perfect work, and His wonderful expectations for us.

Today, many churches have developed the harmful habit of reading the biblical texts in small fragments. If you pay attention, you'll notice that in classes, small groups, preaching, devotionals, and daily reading planners, it has become common practice to read isolated portions of the Bible. This is not necessarily wrong, but if we develop the habit of reading the Bible only in this manner, we run the risk of taking in what we read as snacks and skipping meals, maybe even as if the verses we read are phrases from a horoscope. On the other hand, if we delve into the complete story and take time to notice its details and its application, it helps to ensure that later on we will have a better understanding of those individual texts.

Try this exercise: Ask 10 Christians, of any age, something as simple as, "What is the Bible about?" You will get 10 different answers. Ask them to explain to you how the Old and New Testaments relate and possibly some will begin to hesitate. If you want to go a bit further, ask them to explain to you what the book of Obadiah is about and how it relates to the rest of the Bible and to us today.

These should not be questions that only seminarians or pastors can answer. All believers need to be able to understand them. That is why this material is so important.

The reason for this is very simple. Imagine for a moment a jigsaw puzzle, one that's difficult to put together. Would it have 1,000 pieces? Fifteen hundred? Let's think of a puzzle that has 2,000 pieces and try the following experiment. Imagine now that I take the puzzle box and hide the cover that displays the image we are trying to put together. Then I will ask you to put in your hand randomly and take out only 10 pieces.

Now comes the interesting part: What if I asked you to use those 10 pieces to describe the image? Do you think you'd be able to do it? Of course not! You could make something up, but you certainly would not be able to guess the image as such.

At many churches throughout the continent we asked the same question: What are the most famous biblical texts that all churches know? In every city where we tried this exercise, the response was always the same 10 verses.

Yes, just 20 verses. It appears that our new generations are growing up with only 10 of the 31,130 pieces of the biblical puzzle. And with those 10 verses, we expect them to have a clear picture of God's character, His perfect work, and His expectation toward us. It's impossible. If we base our overall idea on only 10 of the thousands of verses in the Bible, we will undoubtedly develop an image that's false, incomplete, distorted, and disfigured.

Just as it is important to appreciate the fine detail of each piece of the puzzle, it is also indispensable to be able to see the complete picture. And that's what these lessons are about.

We have prepared this book as much as possible as a chronological journey through God's Word, from Genesis to Revelation. It is our hope that once they have an overview of the biblical books, your students will react in two ways.

First, that they'll be able to say, "Now I understand what this book is about!" Each lesson will be effective to the extent that each participant gains a better understanding of the content and purpose of the books of the Bible.

As you will see, since this adventure is designed for a full year of lessons, it is not possible to include all 66 books in 50 weeks. It has been a difficult process to compress, summarize or omit. Moreover, we are convinced that Genesis on its own could take us through 50 weeks! We are confident that we are building a solid foundation, and that we will continue to build on it, with more in-depth studies of the specific books. We are looking forward to what will follow from this.

Second, that by better understanding the full picture, your middle schoolers will now be motivated to learn more about the details. If they can connect each book of the Bible to the complete image of the puzzle, it will make it easier for each individual chapter to make sense. We want to develop devout readers of the Bible, scholars of God's Word. Join them on this tour and help them to explore the richness of each individual biblical passage. Take the time to develop new series about specific books of the Bible, as well as complete biographies of biblical characters.

In addition to considering the maturity and contextual characteristics of each age group, we have chosen a lens with which to look at the books of the Bible in this series. This lens will help us underline the great theological and anthropological themes of the Bible.

Each volume is unique and complementary. Those who travel with us through these four books will certainly have a clear idea of what the Bible is about!

The children's volume was developed around an identity that's outside of this world. The biblical journey will focus on the progressive revelation of God's character. Who is He? How does He present Himself to humans? Knowing God allows us to also know ourselves: What is our natural condition? How is our identity manifested in our behavior? We need to be rescued from our condition, with Jesus Christ being our only hope. To receive Him as Lord and Savior renews us. Who are we now in Christ? How does this transformation manifest itself in our behavior?

The volume for middle schoolers focuses on an unconditional and eternal relationship. The biblical journey will focus on God's initiative to relate to humans. It will highlight the invincible obstacle for man - sin, and Christ's complete victory. The emphasis is on God's faithfulness to man - despite our infidelity - and the closeness that it allows us, only through Christ. What defines God's relationship with us? What should I do to live that relationship today?

The volume for adolescents focuses on crucial decisions. The biblical journey will focus on God's expectations, given our new identity, of lives lived according to His character. We will study the divine perspective in order to make the right decisions in every facet of our lives, the purpose of holiness, and the dire consequences of disobedience. The gospel is not focused on our behavior, but given the Grace of God, our best response is to glorify Him.

The volume for university students is missionary. The biblical journey will focus on God's mission, which seeks to redeem the human being. Special attention will be paid to how God has always fulfilled, and will continue to fulfill until the end, His plan for human beings. Salvation is available to anyone. As part of our new identity, God sends us to explain this gospel to every person, even to the most remote places on the planet. This is our true life's purpose, to live in mission here and now.

On our website, www.e625.com, you will find supplementary material for these lessons. Our goal for the conversations that arise from each lesson is that they be theologically deep and didactically creative.

Of course, all this has been the work of a great team of people involved in the design of the curriculum and instruction. Upon hearing the idea for this series, many friends enthusiastically joined this project. To each of you, THANK YOU for investing in the biblical formation of our new generations!

Let's lead them to know the whole puzzle, to have a biblical image of the person of God, to understand His eternal plan and the response He expects from each one of us.

Let us learn together!

Howard Andruejol and Lucas Leys
General editors

Lesson 1 > WHY IS THE STUDY OF THE WHOLE BIBLE IMPRTANT

Although many believe that the Bible is a single book, we know that it is actually a collection of books written by different authors. Experts in ancient writings and in history have compiled and translated into many languages the 66 books that today make up the collection we call the "Bible."

The Bible may look like an ordinary book, but it is not. It was written by ordinary authors, but its contents are extraordinary, because God Himself is the source of the wisdom and inspiration of everything that's been written in it. That is why so often we refer to the Bible as "the Word of God." There are several reasons why it is very important that we study the Bible as a complete picture from beginning to end, which is what we are going to do with these classes.

The Bible is much more than a history book. The Bible shows how God reveals Himself to human beings. The Bible tells us what God is like and how we can get to know Him, and what His intentions and purpose for us are. In essence it is the history of the relationship between God and the human beings He created.

Note: Middle schoolers are in a time of transition in their mental makeup. They are transitioning from a linear and concrete way of thinking to an abstract and fluctuating way of thinking. As leaders, we must help them to strengthen their thought process based on concrete examples, leading them slowly toward being able to compare and consider different possible scenarios as they interact with each story and book of the Bible. That is why we advise you to have fixed or portable graphics in your classroom, enabling you in each class you to mention the structure of the Bible and the timeframe in which each event occurs. On our website we provide examples of this that you can reproduce.

Welcome and introductory questions on the topic (10 minutes)

Before you start the lesson, and after you greet your pre-adolescents, take three minutes to ask three non-personal questions to help the group get comfortable with one another. These questions can be asked of the whole class, or you can choose someone who you know will feel comfortable answering in front of everyone:

1. What's the purpose of books?
2. What types of books do you like to read? What is your favorite book?
3. What books do you think are important to read?

The stories from the Bible encourage us and fill us with faith. As we learn about the wonders God performed with ordinary people in ancient times, we can grasp that He can also do this with us today. Although the Bible was written thousands of years ago, it is still God's message to us today, and His truth still has the power to change us. When we read and study the Bible, we connect with God's thoughts.

Literature: from boring to fascinating (20 minutes)

Go to the public library in your city (if you don't have a card to check out books, this is a good opportunity for you to get one and start using it!). Ask the librarian for help; it will surely be an adventure for him. Ask him for books from the following categories:

Adventure: Narnia, Lord of the Rings, Superhero books (make sure you don't pick some that might be controversial in your church).
Poetry: Well-known national authors, or a Latino author like Gabriel García Márquez.
Mythology: Hercules, Zeus or some other mythological character.
Biography: A prominent figure from your country: a president, an artist, etc.
Epistles or letters: Often romantic letters are collected during times of war, or from politicians and other prominent figures.
Fables: Short stories, generally about animals.
Treatises: Studies of specific scientific topics, or classics like those of Aristotle or Thomas Aquinas.
Chronicles: Historical facts in chronological order.
Essays: Something like "The Writer and His Ghosts" by Ernesto Sábato
Fairy Tales: Cinderella, Tom Thumb, The Little Prince, etc.

The idea is to have interesting books from as many kinds of literary genres as you can think of. You can also bring children's stories, newspapers, magazines, comic books, romantic novels, etc. You don't need to buy any; the public libraries will have everything.

Take these materials to the class and put them on a large table in the middle of the room. Let the middle schoolers go through all the books and magazines, handle them, take a good look at them, and then ask them:

What kind of books do you see here?
Which one caught your attention the most, and why?

Then take out a Bible and tell them: "Although the Bible appears to be one book, it is actually a collection of books written by many different authors. The Bible is divided as follows..." (Show them the pictures of the books of the Bible. You can do it with the drawings that are in the web attachments, or in any other way that you like).

Download from www.e625.com/lessons the complimentary materials for this section.

Old Testament with 39 books
New Testament with 27 books

The books of the **Old Testament** are divided into five sections and styles:
The Pentateuch (five books): Genesis, Exodus, Leviticus, Numbers, and Deuteronomy (the Law of Moses).
Historical books (12 books): Joshua, Judges, Ruth, 1 and 2 Samuel, 1 and 2 Kings, 1 and 2 Chronicles, Ezra, Nehemiah, and Esther.
Books of poetry or wisdom (five books): Job, Psalms, Proverbs, Ecclesiastes and Songs of Solomon.
Books of the major prophets - so called because they are longer - (five books): Isaiah, Jeremiah, Lamentations, Ezekiel, and Daniel.
Books of the minor prophets - so called because they are shorter - (12 books): Hosea, Joel, Amos, Obadiah, Jonah, Micah, Nahum, Habakkuk, Zephaniah, Haggai, Zechariah, and Malachi.

(The number of each type of book is easy to memorize: 5/12/5/5/12).

The books of the **New Testament** are divided into four sections:
The Gospels: Matthew, Mark, Luke and John.
Historical book: Acts of the Apostles.

Epistles:
1- Paul's thirteen letters:
-Written during his travels: Romans 1 and 2, Corinthians, Galatians 1 and 2, Thessalonians.
-Written from prison: Ephesians, Philippians, Colossians, and Philemon.
-Pastoral letters: 1 and 2 Timothy, Titus.
-(Some would also add Hebrews).
2- General Epistles: James 1 and 2, Peter, 1, 2, and 3 John, and Jude.

Prophetic book: Revelation of John.

The Bible gives answers to everyday questions, tells us how the universe began, how to make good decisions, how to have peace when we are in trouble, how to deal with change, and especially, how to live a life worth living!

Many think of the Bible as an instruction manual: We are God's creation and the Bible is a kind of manual that will help us function at our full potential.

We cannot read only a portion of the Bible because it would be like watching only a few pieces of a movie or only one chapter of a series. Some parts may be funny, but we wouldn't understand where each part of the story fits with the other parts and with the whole. We would be left with only small portions of all that God wants to tell us.

Give each student a copy of "Why Bible Study Is Important" and quickly review all the points in the chart. Then ask two or three students which point they think is the most important and why.

Posters to remember (5 minutes)

Make posters of the following verses, and put them somewhere visible, so students can always read them and engrave them in their hearts. Show them the pictures of the verses and read the words aloud.

Psalms 119:27
Cause me to understand the way of your precepts, that I may meditate on your wonderful deeds.

Psalms 119:105
Your word is a lamp to my feet and a light to my path.

What does it mean to meditate?
To meditate is to think about what we read, so that we can find its meaning and apply it to our lives. The Word of the Lord is what guides us, what gives us strength through His promises, what teaches us the truth, what tells us who God is, what encourages us when we feel discouraged, what gives us faith and teaches us to live a life according to the purpose of the one who created us.
But to know all these things, we need to read it and study it. By doing so we will realize that, even though the Bible was written thousands of years ago, we can still find it relevant and learn from it today.

Pointer (15 minutes)

Give your pre-adolescents materials to prepare a bookmark with the following psalm.

You can prepare strips of cardboard with a hole on the edge and a ribbon or piece of wool.

Bring anything you can get your hands on to decorate. You can ask some parents to help you with the material.

Then print the psalm, one copy for each middle schooler, so they can stick it on bookmarks.

Psalms 119:9-16
How can a young person stay on the path of purity?
By living according to your word.
I seek you with all my heart;
do not let me stray from your commands.
I have hidden your word in my heart
that I might not sin against you.
Praise be to you, Lord;
teach me your decrees.
With my lips I recount
all the laws that come from your mouth.
I rejoice in following your statutes
as one rejoices in great riches.
I meditate on your precepts
and consider your ways.
I delight in your decrees;
I will not neglect your word.

Close with a prayer, asking the Lord that in all the lessons to come He will be the one who reveals His truth to them, the one who ignites the Spirit in your students, so that together they can discover God's secrets and plans.

Download the daily "Family" readings from www.e625.com/lessons.

The word Genesis means "start" or "beginning," and the book of Genesis speaks of many beginnings: the beginning of the universe, the beginning of humans, the beginning of sin and suffering, and also the beginning of a nation and the beginning of God's plan to rescue humans. Like the good beginning of a great story, the main characters are introduced and developed:

- God, making everything happen by creating the universe and human beings in a display of power and glory.
- Satan, trying to ruin everything, makes his appearance starting in chapter three; we'll see him involved in the story again and again until the book of Revelation.
- The first family of the Bible: Adam, Eve, Cain, and Abel.
- Other important characters appear in this first book, including Noah, Abraham and Sarah, Isaac, Jacob and his children, and Joseph.

Genesis deals with issues that go far beyond the kingdom and beyond science. The author (we believe it is Moses) attempts to bring readers closer to the eternal God, revealing His sacred existence and His purpose for us.

Welcome and introductory questions (10 minutes or, ideally, 5 minutes)

Before starting the lesson and after greeting your middle schoolers, take three minutes to ask three non-personal questions, designed to be inviting and unintimidating. These can be directed toward the whole class, or you can call on someone you know will be comfortable answering in front of the whole group:

1. If you had to take three people on a trip across the country, who would you take?
2. If you could be the creator of any invention, which one would you choose and why?
3. What quality impresses you the most: Honesty (truth in spite of), faithfulness (permanence in spite of), or mercy (even if it's not deserved)? Why?

Today we will begin with the beginning of all things. We will discover God's purpose in creating everything, and especially in creating us to be His partners in adventure. We will also discover some of His most outstanding qualities.

Say it with art (20 minutes)

This is a variation of the old show and tell game that will greatly entertain pre-adolescents. Divide your group into four small groups. Have a bag and pieces of paper with four different animal names ready. Once you know the number of participants that day, place equal amounts of each of the four animal types inside the bag, mix them up, and let everyone choose a piece of paper. Have students join with the others who drew the same animal they did, forming the four teams. Note: Never force anyone to be part of a group, especially if they are new or visiting. If the teams are too uneven, send a leader to be part of a smaller or unevenly matched group. You will need a blackboard and chalk (or blank sheets of papers and markers), dough (clay, play dough, etc.), and three cards: one with the word "mime," another with the word "sculpture," and the third with the word "drawing." Lastly, you'll need a bag with pieces of paper with words for the teams to represent and guess: animals, objects from nature, elements of creation (boat, rhinoceros, etc.). If it seems too easy, you can add a bag with qualifying adjectives such as happy, sad, bouncy, etc., which will make the game funnier.

When it comes to the sculpture do not use adjectives because it will take too much time. They will only have 30-40 seconds to represent the words in most categories. The sculptures will take 60 seconds.

We advise that there be no more than four teams. If your group is very large, you can divide it into boys and girls and then divide into smaller groups, or you can have a small group of participants come to the front and interact with the audience, or have a leader guide the activity for two teams.

Once you have the groups formed, have the first participant come forward. First, she must choose, without looking, one of the three cards to determine how she must represent the word (mime, sculpture or drawing) and show it to her team. Then, without looking, she will take from the bag the thing she has to represent (object of creation). Next, if you choose, you can have her choose a qualifying adjective for said object of creation.

She might get something like "drawing," "bear," and "bouncy"; or "mime," "monkey," and "in love." The possibilities are infinitely hilarious; just use your imagination! Remember that for the sculpture it will be easier if your player just chooses from the first bag and doesn't pick an adjective. Then all you have to do is sit back and enjoy your pre-adolescents' imaginations. Take photos or videos if you want to capture the fun!

After the game, you can play a song or video about creation, such as a few minutes of this: **https://youtu.be/asC27KnW3wE?si=8C_1lmKzDPnC5lOe**

Book review (20 minutes)

Pre-adolescents who have been in church for a long time will probably be thinking "not again!" when they hear that you will be talking about Genesis in this lesson. But this time we are not going to tell the story of Adam and Eve, or Moses, or the flood. We are going to look at a general snapshot of all of Genesis, and we are going to challenge them to remember the stories that they've learned as children. For those who have never been to Sunday School before it will be fun, helping them gain an initial understanding and helping them know more of what the book of Genesis is about for the future.

Take the summary from the beginning of the lesson. Print or make boxes with the key words that make up the thread of the story (or use drawings or images that represent the story) to help your pre-adolescents pay attention. Ask questions and pause so they can use their brains. If they don't respond quickly, give them the answer and continue with the story.

BEGINNING - UNIVERSE - HUMANITY - SIN - SUFFERING - PLAN - GOD - SATAN - EGYPT

The word Genesis means "start" or "beginning," and the book of Genesis speaks of many beginnings: the beginning of the universe, the beginning of humans, the beginning of sin and suffering, but also the beginning of a nation and the beginning of God's plan to rescue humans. Like the good beginning of any great story, the main characters are introduced and developed. God, making everything happen by creating the universe and human beings in a display of power and glory. Satan, trying to ruin everything, makes his appearance starting in chapter three, and we'll see him involved in the story again and again until the book of Revelation (and still today). Genesis tells us about the first family of the Bible: Adam, Eve, Cain, and Abel, and also about the first great natural disaster: Noah and the flood. In Genesis there are a lot of "firsts" in human history, and the book ends with the death of Joseph in"Egypt. We will begin meeting some of the most important characters with the following activity.

The most important stories

Have your middle schoolers return to the same groups they formed earlier. Each team will receive the name of one of the important people in the story and the related biblical quotes. They will create a poster that captures everything about the character: family, work, and etc. For example, for Abraham the poster might include an altar with a sheep.

Group 1- Abraham: the promise of the impossible. Gen. 12:1-5; 15:1-6; 18:1, 9-14; 21:1-7.
Group 2- Isaac: obedience brings blessing. Gen. 22:1-12; 25:19-26.

Group 3- Jacob: the power of the blessing. Gen. 26:34; 27:33; 30:22-24.
Group 4- Joseph : integrity and forgiveness. Gen. 37:3-11, 37:23-28; 39:1-5; 42:6-10; 45:1-9.

Give the groups 10 minutes to read, cut, paste, and put together the story. Everyone must show their work, and at the end you will show what each group has done as an art exhibition.

Closing (5 minutes)

God reveals Himself in many ways throughout the Bible. Some stories seem a little strange or hard to believe, but in all of them God shows us His character. His desire is that we can get to know Him in such a way that we will be able to recognize Him working in our lives today.

In Genesis:

God reveals Himself in creation: He reveals His love by creating us, and He shows His interest by relating to us as a father.

God is faithful and always keeps His promises: Abraham was old, but he believed God, and God kept His promises. Although Abraham was not the one who had thousands of children, the history of a nation began with him.

God shows His grace: Abraham believed God and obeyed Him despite His difficult request. God wanted to show His grace toward Abraham and Isaac, but to do so He needed Abraham's trust and faith.

God is merciful: Joseph remained faithful to God and always strove to be the best, even in the worst situations. God had mercy on Joseph and blessed him in everything he did. Joseph recognized God's mercy and was able to be merciful to his brothers.

Download the daily "Family" readings from www. e625.com/lessons.

The word Exodus means departure or exit, and refers to the departure of the Hebrews from Egypt. Exodus tells the story of the Israelites, starting right where Genesis ended. The people of Israel, who had been received by Pharaoh during the time of Joseph, have now become a nation of slaves, hated by their rulers.

Pharaoh tries to control this rapidly multiplying people, but God has a rescue plan prepared with a special name: Moses. The liberation of Israel from the hands of the Egyptians is only the beginning of a much greater plan, a plan of redemption, adoption, and the development of a nation chosen as God's people. Although we will focus only on the books of Genesis, Exodus, and Leviticus, the books of Numbers and Deuteronomy also include norms and laws that we will study in this lesson. Take a look at these books and read through them to gain a better understanding of how they are linked to each other. Because they are connected, these first five books are called the Pentateuch or "the Law."

Welcome and introductory questions (10 minutes)

Before starting the lesson and after greeting your middle schoolers, take three minutes to ask three non-personal questions, designed to be inviting and unintimidating. These can be directed toward the whole class, or you can call on someone you know will be comfortable answering in front of the whole group:

1. If you had to go to another city or another country with your whole family right now, where would you go and why?
2. If you had the opportunity to build a house, what would it be like (rooms, game-room, swimming pool, etc.)?
3. If you were the owner of the house, what rules would you set?

To quickly tell the story of the exodus we will ask some students to act out the story. Choose the characters, trying to pick people you know won't be embarrassed to act a little.

If you want, you can prepare name tags with the roles each student will play. As you delegate the roles, each student can stick theirs to their chest.

Variation: If you don't have too many students, you can adapt this activity using drawings. Cut pictures of people from magazines, draw your own clothing, and dress them as Egyptians and Jews from those times. Have fun making the voices!

Keep in mind that attention spans are short; move this activity along quickly to keep students engaged. They will pay attention to the story and act spontaneously as they listen to you.

Characters:
> Pharaoh: a leader
> Baby Moses: a baby doll and crib
> Moses' mother
> Moses' sister
> Pharaoh's daughter
> Guard
> Moses
> Aaron
> Zipporah and her sisters.
> The people of Israel: the rest of the students

Tales of an escape
As you read the story, the characters have to spontaneously act out what you say. Have moments of silence so they can repeat a phrase or react to what they have to do. Let them be creative! Remember to read energetically and keep this activity moving along quickly.

Story I (5 minutes)

After Joseph died, in the book of Genesis, the Jews who stayed to live in Egypt multiplied greatly (students make "pop" noises). A new king arrived in Egypt who had not met Joseph, and he was afraid that the Jews would get out of control (students act out of control). So Pharaoh forced the Hebrews to do all kinds of forced labor (Pharaoh punishes the Hebrews), especially in construction, as well as other types of slave labor. He also ordered: "Throw all the male babies of the Jews into the river." It was then that Moses was born and his mother hid him for three months. When she could no longer hide him, she wove him a basket and put him in the river. Then Pharaoh's daughter went down to bathe in the river and found Moses in the basket, and saved him from being killed. She adopted him and took him with her to her palace.

One day, when Moses had grown up, he went to see his blood brothers and saw that a guard was whipping them (a guard mistreats the crowd). Moses hit the guard and killed him, and hid him in the sand (Joseph kills the guard). The news of what had happened spread very quickly. When Pharaoh found out he planned to kill Moses, so Moses fled Egypt. Arriving in Midian, Moses again became the defender of the poor. He helped some women who were being bothered by some shepherds. The women told their father what Moses had done, and their father received Moses into his house. Moses married one of the girls, Zipporah. One day, when Moses was taking his father-in-law's sheep to pasture, he saw that a bush was on fire but was not being burned up. As he approached the bush, it called to him: "Moses! Moses!" Moses got closer. The burning bush, which was God, said to him: "Take off your sandals, because you are treading on holy ground. I am the God of your Fathers, I am the God of Abraham, Isaac, and Jacob. I saw my people suffering, I know their sorrows well" (act as suffering people). "So, I will deliver them from the Egyptians and bring them into a good and spacious land. I will send you to Pharaoh to bring the Israelites out of Egypt." To which Moses replied: "Why me?" God said, "Fear not, I will be with you." God also sent Aaron to meet Moses and help him confront Pharaoh. Finally, Moses and Aaron came to Pharaoh and said, "This is what the Lord, the God of Israel, says: 'Let my people go so that they may celebrate a feast in my honor in the wilderness.'" And Pharaoh answered, "Who is the Lord? And why do you distract the people from their labor?" He drove them out of his presence and gave more work to the Jews, who became angry with Moses (crowd boos).

Moses complained to God and doubted his intentions but God responded, "Now you are going to see what I am going to do with Pharaoh. Only through my powerful hand will Pharaoh let the people leave, only through my powerful hand will he drive them out of his country; And when I display my power against Egypt and bring out the Israelites from there, they will know that I AM the Lord."

The plagues of confusion (5 minutes)
Ask for two or more volunteers to come forward.

In the telling of the story we reached the point where Moses listened to God but Pharaoh refused, and made the work of the Jews more difficult. But God had promised that the Egyptians would see His power and that because of what He would do, Pharaoh would let God's people go. What happened next? God had to send 10 plagues until Pharaoh finally let the Israelites leave.

On a table, place a set of 10 papers with the 10 plagues written on them (make more than one set if you're dividing your students into teams), each paper with a piece of tape on the back. One representative per team must come to the front and prepare to arrange the 10 plagues in the order that they happened. The rest of the team will help their representative place the plagues in the correct order. In one minute the representative must tape the 10 plagues on the board or wall in the order they think is most accurate. The team that gets the most correct will be the winner.

Story II (5 minutes)

(The story continues using the same characters.)
Finally, after the worst plague of all, which was the death of all the firstborn in every family that had not marked the doors of their house with the blood of a lamb, Pharaoh, who had also lost his firstborn, let Israel go (crowd beats the ground with their feet). A column of clouds guided them during the day and a column of fire at night to show them which way they should go to reach the promised land. When they had been on their way for several days, Pharaoh regretted letting the Israelites go: "What did I do? Who is going to do the forced labor?" he wondered. He got his horses and went after the Jews. The Israelites, who found themselves facing the Red Sea, felt betrayed and had no escape, but God had a plan. The columns that were ahead moved to the back of the crowd, in between the Jews and the Egyptians. Then Moses extended his arm over the sea. A strong wind divided the waters in two. When all the Israelites finished crossing the sea, Moses extended his arm again, and the waters closed, destroying the Egyptians who came after him and the Israelites.

With the Egyptians out of the picture, the Israelites set out on the true path. Moses encountered many difficulties while traveling with so many people, but God was always with them. On one occasion, God called Moses and asked him to go up to Mount Sinai, where God gave him new instructions for the new people.

The Ten Commandments (5 minutes)

A new opportunity to play: Now ask two or more players to go to the front of the group. In the same way as they did before, they must now place the 10 commandments in order. The entire team will help their representatives put as many commandments as possible in the corresponding order in one minute or less.

Story III (5 minutes)

(The story continues using the same characters).

When Moses finally came back down from Mount Sinai with the tablets of the Ten Commandments and a few other instructions, he found that the Israelites had screwed up and had built themselves a golden calf, which they were worshiping it (people worshiping). Moses got angry, threw the tablets of the commandments at them, and beat the golden calf to dust! Then he again went up the mountain. God again wrote the tablets and the terms of the covenant with His people.

Finally, God's people came together, built the sanctuary just as God commanded it, and the Spirit of God descended on it like a cloud of glory. When the cloud lifted, the Israelites broke camp and walked toward where God moved.

Conclusion (10 minutes)

This is the story of God and Moses, but it is also the beginning of the story of a people chosen by God. This story started with the Israelites but continues with us; it's also our story (6:7).

It is the story of a man who, although he doubted many times and asked God not to be the one to free Israel from Egypt, was obedient. That is why Moses was chosen to be part of God's great plan for His people (7:6). God formed a friendly relationship with Moses (19:20; 24:1-2,12; 33:11).

In Genesis, God promised Abraham offspring as numerous as the stars in the sky or the sand of the sea, and in Exodus what began with one man ended with millions of Jews walking to occupy their own territory. **God fulfills his promises (6:8).**

It is the story of a people who, although they were unfaithful to God on many occasions, were loved by God. He chose them, and wanted to be their God. He is a **God of mercy**, who saw the suffering of His people and heard their prayers (3:7; 6:5-6).

The plagues were a display of God's power (6:1; 14:4) to leave no doubt that He was the true God (8:19), who was unlike anything they had seen before.

The Ten Commandments were rules for coexistence between the people who would form a new nation. God loves us more than anyone, and His advice is always good.

Then the Lord came down in the cloud and stood there with Moses and proclaimed His name, the Lord. And He passed in front of Moses, proclaiming: *The Lord, the Lord, the compassionate and gracious God, slow to anger, abounding in love and faithfulness, maintaining love to thousands, and forgiving wickedness, rebellion and sin* (34:5-7, NIV).

Download the daily "Family" readings from www. e625.com/lessons.

The book of Leviticus gets its name because it refers to everything "pertaining to the Levites." The Levites were the tribe of Levi, one of the twelve sons of Jacob, and were in charge of priestly duties. The book received this name because particular emphasis is given to priestly functions for people's approach to God in a holy and reverent manner.

The book of Exodus ends with the construction of the sanctuary, and it's the instruction manual for how they should use the temple. During this entire period, the people of Israel remained in the same place, learning to obey and please God. It is a kind of code of holiness, to be able to enter into God's presence and worship Him. The instructions in Leviticus were revealed by God to Moses (who was also from the tribe of Levi). This book shows us how meticulous God is and how imperfect humans are. With such rigid norms, we can understand in greater depth the wonderful work of Jesus Christ on the cross as a perfect and eternal sacrifice, through which today we have direct access to the presence of the Holiest One.

Welcome and introductory questions (10 minutes)

Before starting the lesson and after greeting your middle schoolers, take three minutes to ask three non-personal questions, designed to be inviting and unintimidating. These can be directed toward the whole class, or you can call on someone you know will be comfortable answering in front of the whole group:

1. Have you ever gone to a new school, or moved to a new city, and had to make new friends?
2. What characteristics do good friends have?
3. What helps us to continue being good friends with the friends we already have? What helps us with those we don't see as often?

After they left Egypt and started wandering through the desert, God spoke with Moses, and they remained in the same place for some time, at the foot of Mount Sinai, where God gave them the Ten Commandments and the laws of justice and mercy (Ex. 20 and 23). The book of Exodus ends with God's instructions regarding the building of the tabernacle and the consecration of Aaron and his sons to make them priests (Ex. 28-29). Thus Aaron became the first priest of Israel.

Aaron (Moses' brother) and Aaron's sons were from the tribe of Levi. From then on, the priests always had to be chosen from the tribe of Levi. The name of this book means "belonging to the Levites."

The book of Leviticus includes God's instructions on how sacrifices were to be presented, how priests were to perform their duties, and how the people were to remain clean before God.

Important friends (30 minutes)

Divide your students into small groups. Let them join with their best friends, and then assign others so that there are four or five per group. Choose one student to be the one who leads the discussion, and give them the following instructions: They can only discuss each question for five minutes, so they must start quickly, and speak briefly. When the five minutes are up, signal the group leaders to move on to the next question. The leader can decide who will answer first, and if everyone wants to answer a question, the leader should make time for as many people as possible to do so.

Assign one student in each group to take notes. These don't need to be detailed, but just brief notes to be able to remember and share with the larger group what was said. Then give each group a copy of the following questionnaire:

Download the complimentary materials for this section from www.e625.com/lessons.

Closing (15 minutes)

After quickly going over their answers, finish as follows:
In Leviticus, God gave the people a long list of sacrifices, laws, and commandments to fulfill. He did this for two reasons. One was to enable the people to understand how special God is, and that they should honor Him. The other reason is that God wanted His people to learn to get closer to Him and get to know Him better, so He could be closer to them. Through His commandments, God helped them to live better, to become better people, and to become holy as He is holy. Furthermore, the Lord was preparing the way for the future, a time when everyone would need Jesus, the only one who could fulfill all the rules and thus give us free entry into God's presence without the need for sacrifices. Jesus was the perfect sacrifice who erased all of man's evil by forgiving us and reconciling us with God.

If any of you has understood the importance and need to get closer to God, to let Him be our good friend who watches over us, protects us, and loves us, this is the time to get closer to Him with a sincere heart.

Close with a prayer recognizing who God is and all His power, and at the same time His desire to be our God. For those who want to participate, lead a prayer of surrender and reconciliation with God.

Download from www.e625.com/lessons the complimentary materials for this section.

Lesson 5 > JOSHUA

Joshua is the first book in the biblical category we call "historical books." The story picks up right where Deuteronomy ends. After the death of Moses, command is given to Joshua. Without a doubt God, and also Moses, knew that they could trust Joshua because Joshua had demonstrated beforehand that he trusted God and respected authorities. In the book of Numbers we can see that Joshua was one of the 12 spies who first went to check out the promised land. Although they saw the giants, he and his friend Caleb were the only two who did not cower. That is why God's first order to Joshua was to finally take the promised land. Up to this point, Israel had wandered for 40 years in the desert, but this time what had been promised would be fulfilled. The book of Joshua tells us of all the battles that led to conquering the promised land, finally ending with the death of Joshua at 110 years of age. Joshua was a great leader who knew how to love God, fulfill His commandments, and lead a great people to conquest.

Welcome and introductory questions (5 minutes)

Before starting the lesson and after greeting your middle schoolers, take three minutes to ask three non-personal questions, designed to be inviting and unintimidating. These can be directed toward the whole class, or you can call on someone you know will be comfortable answering in front of the whole group:

1. If you could choose today what type of work you will eventually do, what would you choose?
2. Do you know anyone who works in this field, and perhaps could be your role model?
3. Is there anything you learn more about or work on today that would help you to do well in this career someday?

We all have hopes and dreams for the future. Over time those ideas change as we discover new abilities and talents, and as our interests change. Technology and the world's needs also continue to change, and future options change along with them.

Nevertheless, it is smart to develop our talents from a young age, continue to learn new things, and investigate many possibilities so that when our time comes, we can be the best in the work we pursue.

Opening video (5 minutes)

Play the following clip as an opening to the theme of the book.
https://www.youtube.com/watch?v=nfmhORqNaco

It's under the title "Karate Kid: (Columbia Pictures Industries 1984), result of training. The video is 7:22 minutes long, but in this first part you will stop it at 3:48, when it says, "come back tomorrow."

Here, Mr. Miyagi trains Daniel by having him paint and sand and wax. The video starts just as he is finishing painting the house. Mr. Miyagi appears with a fishing rod, and Daniel complains about all the work Mr. Miyagi is making him do. The first part to show students lasts until the 3:48 mark. The second part begins right where the first one ends, ending at the beach scene where Mr. Miyagi breaks the top of the beer bottles with a single blow, completing 7:22. You can show this to your group later if time permits.

We would all like to be the hero or to have some extraordinary ability, but for the most part, people don't like doing the hard work needed to learn special skills. However, with effort and preparation we can become excellent at anything we choose to do.

Joshua's preparation (10 minutes)

In Joshua, God fulfills His promise to free the Israelites from the hands of the Egyptians and to lead them to their own prosperous and abundant land, where they would become a nation. But in order to accomplish this, and all the extraordinary stories that God made happen through Joshua, he needs to prepare to become the leader God's people need.

In the books of Numbers and Deuteronomy, we can see how the Lord begins to prepare Joshua to fulfill his purpose.

For this lesson, prepare some posters or print-outs in advance with words highlighted in the text. You can stick them on a blackboard or on a wall.

1- Have someone read Exodus 17:9-12. Joshua was Moses' assistant and although it was a great privilege, sometimes living in the shadow of a great leader is not much fun. Often, Joshua accompanied Moses to meet with God, but he always had to stay outside the party waiting for Moses. Moses asked Joshua to choose some men to fight against the Amalekites, who were coming to attack them.

When Moses raised his hands the Israelites were winning, but when he got tired and put them down the Amalekites were winning. In verse 14, the Lord makes sure that Joshua finds out how they won the battle. The Lord was showing Joshua His faithfulness, how He acted, while increasing Joshua's faith. **Joshua showed courage and submission to authority.**

2- Have someone read Numbers 13:2-3. The Lord ordered Moses to send several men to explore the land the Lord had promised them. After 40 days they returned to report what they saw, and described a very good land with many fruits, but...a land that was full of giants and surrounded by many other nations of people they'd have to fight. Everyone became discouraged and began to complain: "Why did we leave Egypt?" But along with Moses and Aaron were two of the **explorers**: Caleb and Joshua. They tried to encourage the people by telling them that with the Lord they could conquer the earth. However, because of the people's complaints, none of those over 20 years old were ever able to see the promised land, other than Caleb and Joshua, who were able to because of their courage and trust in the Lord. In Numbers 14:6-8 and 30 **Joshua shows that** he learned his lesson about faith. He **trusts in God**. He also shows bravery and patriotism by taking risks for everyone along with his companions.

3- Have someone else read Numbers 27:18-23. The Lord was already granting Joshua authority. He told him to be anointed, so that when he orders the people to go to war, everyone will follow him, and when he makes them come back, they will all come back. Joshua was still under the leadership of Moses but the Lord was already starting to give him **authority** through his faith and obedience. **Joshua showed humility** by staying under Moses' orders, even though he had a lot of authority.

4- In Deuteronomy 31:23, the Lord **affirmed** Joshua by telling him to be brave, that he would lead the people to the promised land. God promised to be with Joshua. Joshua received a purpose that would be fulfilled in the future; He **knew how to wait** while he continued to fulfill his role. God was preparing him.

5- Finally, in Deuteronomy 34:9, God filled Joshua with **wisdom** and the Israelites obeyed him. Under his leadership they did everything the Lord had commanded them. God gave him the final touch Joshua needed to be a good leader: wisdom. Joshua remained faithful to the Lord in all situations. **Joshua was a wise leader.**

How many times have you thought you are not capable, you are too small or insignificant, or that the tasks given to you are too small? Whenever you think this way, remember that giving your best, being patient, and waiting on God will lead to the best results. Like Joshua, sometimes you may be under the leadership of your mom and dad or an adult, but that doesn't mean God doesn't see you. He thinks about you and is making plans for you.

Note: If you spent less than 10 minutes on this section of the lesson, you can show the last part of the video, starting right where you paused it at 3:48, to see the next step of the Karate Kid's training.

Rock, paper, scissors... and sticks (20 minutes)
Divide your group into two teams.

Materials needed: sticks and straws (although you can replace them with another element).

Each group must form a circle, an inner one looking outward and an outer one looking inward. All players in the inner circle must have three sticks (or something similar). On the count of three, all players must face an opponent from the other circle and play a round of the traditional rock, paper, scissors. Every time a player in the inner circle loses, they must hand one of the sticks to the outer player. After the first round, the players in the outer circle will now compete against the person one to the right of their original opponent. Again they play rock, paper, scissors. If the inside circle player loses, they must hand over a stick. If they tie, they rotate without anything happening. If the person in the inner circle wins, they do not need to hand over the stick. When an inner circle player gives up the third stick, they must leave the circle, and the outside player will go to the center of both circles. The goal is to get all the inner circle players out as quickly as possible. The game must be fast and quick, with everyone simultaneously shouting "rock, paper, scissors," playing the game, and rotating. If someone has to come in or go out, they should do so quickly without stopping the game.

Keep time, and stop the game after five minutes. Count how many members of the inner circle are still playing. Then, have the teams swap: the inner circle is now the outer circle, and the outer circle is now the inner circle (and they have the sticks). Repeat the game. After another five minutes, count how many players remain in the inner circle. The group that ended up with the most players still in the inner circle wins. When time is up everyone can go back to their seats.

The most outstanding stories (15 minutes)
Have students gather in groups of two or three and give them the following verses to read. Always think strategically when handing out readings. They are short readings of 6 to 15 verses. It won't take more than five minutes to read them. To make it very quick, have the verses written on pieces of paper to hand out.

The Adventures of Joshua:
Group 1- Joshua 3:5-17: the crossing of the Jordan River.
Group 2- Joshua 6:3-17 and 6:20-21: the conquest of Jericho.
Group 3- Joshua 8:3-8, 8:18-20, and 8:26: obedience and victory.
Group 4- Joshua 10:9-15: the hail, the sun and the moon.
Group 5- Joshua 11:16-23: promises fulfilled.

Group 6- Joshua 13:1 and 6-7 and 23:1-8: Joshua's end.

After groups finish reading, following the order above, ask them to sum up the story that they read with the large group. Ask them to be very brief, or set a timer and challenge them to tell the story in one minute.

Closing (5 minutes)

Joshua was a faithful follower of the Lord, brave and loyal. The Lord rewarded him with much more than he could have imagined. With Joshua, God's people finally became an organized nation with a territory. God used Joshua to fulfill many of His most important promises. Joshua knew how to submit, learn, and be faithful to God and his leaders, and the Lord used him in great ways.

His adventures were quite similar to the adventures of Moses, Obviously the Lord prepared Joshua so that he could face difficulties and challenges. Many times we ask ourselves, what does the Lord want for me? Taking advantage of the opportunities that are presented today, getting involved, taking on the challenges, obeying and being faithful to the Lord will take us to places we could not imagine. The Lord will prepare us to fulfill His plans, but first we need a humble heart willing to serve Him in any circumstance.

Closing video: to show that effort and dedication lead to good results, you can show them the end of the movie The Karate Kid:
https://www.youtube.com/watch?v=QqWClxG0eOw
under the title "Karate Kid, the final fight of the tournament."

This clip lasts about five minutes. It begins with the two finalists in their last fight, ready inside the circle, and ends with the presentation of the trophy celebrating Daniel's victory.

Download the daily "Family" readings from www. e625.com/lessons.

Judges

After Joshua died, having conquered almost all the territory, and organized the people of Israel by tribe (each in its designated territory), things became quite normal and routine. At first the Israelites continued taking possession of the land, but when Joshua's entire generation died, a new one arose that did not know the Lord or what He had done for Israel.

They adopted the customs and gods of the people they had conquered. God was furious with them, but still gave them several opportunities by providing them with leaders, or judges. While these judges led the people, there was peace and God blessed them, but once the leader died, they soon returned to doing evil before the Lord, and great consequences befell them.

Ruth

The period of the judges was a dark time for the people of Israel. The lack of leadership, wars, and idolatry, due to mixing with other cultures, weakened Israel politically and spiritually: "...everyone did what he wanted" (Judges 17:6). Among so much immorality, Ruth's story is refreshing and encouraging. It's a story of love, loyalty, and faith, and it's with remembering. Ruth was a Moabite, married to an Israelite. When she became a widow, instead of returning to her home in search of a new husband, she decided to follow her mother-in-law, Naomi, to Bethlehem. Once there, Ruth has a love story, and marries Boaz. They have a son named Obed, a grandson named Jesse, and a great-grandson named David, King David. Ruth's story begins dark and uncertain, but ends with a bright future: King David and the dynasty of none other than Jesus.

Welcome and introductory questions (10 minutes)

Before starting the lesson and after greeting your middle schoolers, take three minutes to ask three non-personal questions, designed to be inviting and unintimidating. These can be directed toward the whole class, or you can call on someone you know will be comfortable answering in front of the whole group:

1. When someone does something bad to us once and we decide to forgive them, how does it make us feel?
2. If that same person does something bad to us over and over again, how does he make us feel? Do we have to forgive them every time?
3. Is God obligated to forgive us every time we commit a sin? Why do we believe that God has no difficulty in forgiving? Is it God's obligation to forgive?

Forgiving is not easy, but when we do it, it makes us feel good. And we feel even better when someone we offended forgives us, truly forgives us, setting aside what we did. What's more difficult is having to forgive someone who continues to hurt us over and over in the same way—with a lie, with a betrayal, ignoring us, etc. The Israelites did this to God all the time, but God was merciful. He is our best example of forgiveness and true love.

Three important points:

1- The book of Judges begins just after Joshua died. God's people turned away from Him again and again. This caused them to make very poor decisions, and the consequences fell on them without mercy.
Read: Judges 2:7, 10-14.

2- When the people found themselves in trouble because the Lord left them at the mercy of the people around them and with whom they had mixed, they were repentant and begged the Lord to deliver them. Their false gods could never do anything for them because they were not real.

Read: Judges 2:1-3 (the same thing happens again in Judges 6:7-10—it seems like they had very poor memories!).

3- Through different characters, leaders, and prophets, God rescued the people from their wrong way of living and then they returned to God. But as soon as any given leader died, the people once again followed other gods and returned to misfortune.

Read Judges 2:16-19.

> Why did people forget about God?
> Why did they prefer to worship other gods?
> Although sometimes we know about God and hear the things He did and still does today, many times we forget about Him and behave as if He is not real. Why does this happen to us?
> What examples can we think of?

While the people of Israel were going through all these ups and downs in their faith, the Bible also teaches us about the faith and courage of a woman from another nation, Moab. Her name was Ruth. Unlike the people of God, Ruth knew how to value faithfulness and honor, and God used her so that everyone would know her story. Among Ruth's descendants there would be a higher honor than she could have ever hoped for. Her great-grandson would be King David, and from her genealogy the Savior, Jesus, would be born.

Interview (20 minutes)

Separate candies of two flavors into equal parts. When all the students are gathered, ask them to sit on the floor or gather in a circle. Then throw all the candies up. Then, form two groups according to the type of candy they have grabbed. From these two large groups, make four by dividing the girls and the boys (if you don't have too many students, just divide them into girls and boys).

You will need a blank sheet of paper and a pencil, a Bible, a poster or cardboard, and colors.

Give the boys the following stories, one for each group:
"Gideon" (Judges 6:1-10, 36-40; 7:1-22) and "Samson" (Judges 16:2-31).

Give the girls the following stories:
Ruth meets Boaz (Ruth 1:18-2:23) and Ruth marries Boaz (Ruth 3:1-9 and 16-18, 4:1-6 and 9-10 and 13-17).

Each group must read their story and choose someone to represent the main character. Then they should prepare questions as if they were going to do a red carpet interview before the premiere of a movie. Anything else you want to add is fine. They must ask at least five questions to help us learn more about the story that they read. In addition, provide each group with posters and markers so that they can prepare a movie-type poster about their story.

Closing (5 minutes)

God makes it clear through the stories in Judges and in Ruth that He loves His people, that He is willing to forgive them again and again even when they fall into the same error each time. God always calls brave people who love Him so they can remind the people that He is the true God and that He always protects them and rescues them, even when it seems impossible. The history of Israel is our history, too, because we are part of God's people. But even knowing what God did for us and hearing what he does today, we still forget over and over. We forget Him and put our interest in things that have no real value.

God wants to use us if we are willing to follow and obey Him. Like Ruth, if we remain faithful even in difficult times and honor Him with our lives, we will not only be called God's people, but He will prepare something very special for us.

Download the daily "Family" readings from www. e625.com/lessons.

Samuel was tasked with leading the Israelites when they left the time of the judges and entered the time of the kings. He established the office of the prophet and developed it to the level of priesthood and royalty. From that time on, the prophets promoted and sustained the spiritual guidance of Israel as instruments of God, to communicate His will. Samuel was a miracle for Hannah, a barren woman who, upon having him, dedicated him to God in gratitude. Eli, who was the priest at that time, raised Samuel in the temple.

God called Samuel and used him as the spiritual leader of Israel. After many years in which he led Israel toward the Lord, the people of Israel asked Samuel for an earthly king: God was not enough for them. Samuel anointed the first king of Israel, who was called Saul, and thus Samuel became the last of Israel's judges. The book of 1 Samuel ends with the death of Saul and 2 Samuel and covers the coronation of David, and tells the great stories of David as king.

Welcome and introductory questions (5 minutes)

Before starting the lesson and after greeting your middle schoolers, take three minutes to ask three non-personal questions, designed to be inviting and unintimidating. These can be directed toward the whole class, or you can call on someone you know will be comfortable answering in front of the whole group:

1. If you could choose a position in government, which one would you want to hold?
2. What would a country be like without a president?
3. Why do you think we need to change presidents from time to time

The Israelites had never had a king. They had had great leaders like Moses who had led them out of Egypt, Joshua who had organized them, and the judges who had guided them in matters of the laws and the Lord's commandments. The last of these judges was Samuel, and he was the priest and prophet of God who gave Israel its first king: Saul. This was the beginning of a new stage in the Hebrew nation, with new adventures and stories being written.

The king's ring (10 minutes)

For this activity you will need a rope or thick thread and one or two small rings that fit in the palm of your hand. All players will stand in a circle holding the rope. Before tying it up to close the circle, pass the rope through the ring(s) so that they can rotate in a circle around the rope. One or two players must be inside the circle.

On the count of three, each ring must begin to circulate from hand to hand in such a way that the players in the center cannot know where it is. For this, all players must pretend to have the ring and move their hands from one side to the other without releasing the rope to confuse the players in the center. After 15 seconds everyone must stop and the players in the center will each have one chance to guess who is the king with the ring in his hand. If they guess right, they switch places with the player who had the ring in his hand. If they don't guess correctly, they will remain in the middle and have three chances before their first penalty or punishment.

Main ideas in 1 and 2 Samuel (25 minutes)

As you recite the passages, let the characters act spontaneously. If the reading says, "God called him: Samuel, Samuel," whoever makes the voice of God must repeat it. If it is a longer sentence, they can say it in their own words so that it is funny and memorable. In this exercise the acting must be fast and the story must be told very quickly for it to be fun.

1- 1 Samuel 3:1-10 and 19-20
Characters you need: Samuel, Eli, and the voice of God.
Question for everyone: What is the story telling us?
Conclusion: How does God call Samuel to serve Him? Samuel did not know the voice of God, but he lived in the temple. We need to be attentive to the voice of God, to listen when He calls us.

2- 1 Samuel 8:1-8
Characters you need: Samuel, the elders of the church (all students), the voice of God.
Pregunta para todos: Question for everyone:
Conclusion: Samuel had no one to inherit his position when he died because his children did not do what was right before God, so the people asked for a king. And although Samuel got angry, God told him: "They don't reject you, they reject me because they don't want me to be their King."

3- 1 Samuel 10:20-27
Characters you need: Samuel, tribes (all students), the voice of God, Saul (the tallest student).
Question for everyone: Why did Saul hide? Why would the people disrespect him?
Conclusion: Saul was from the tribe of Benjamin, which was one of the smallest tribes, and his family was not very large or powerful (1 Sam. 9:21) so he did not feel worthy of being king, and probably many others thought the same way. We do not always believe that we are capable of doing what God asks of us. Later we will see the true key to being a good or a bad leader, regardless of who we are.

4- 1 Samuel 15:10-23
Characters you need: Samuel, the voice of God, Saul (the tallest student).
Question for everyone: Why was God angry with Saul? What is most important to God?
Conclusion: The most important thing in this story is that God wants us to obey Him, and although some things may seem like they are right and would help us or make us look good in front of others, the most important thing is to always obey God's instructions.

5- 1 Samuel 16:1, 5-14, 18-19, 21-23
Characters you need: Samuel, the voice of God, Jesse and his sons (only the three he mentions), and David.
Question for everyone: Saul didn't know that Samuel had anointed a new king, yet David ended up serving Saul. Do you think God had a purpose for David being with the king?
Conclusion: Often we do not understand the coincidences or situations that happen to us, but God has a purpose to form us, train us, and accomplish His plans for us, as long as we are willing to obey.

Finishing the books (10 minutes)

What is David's best-known story? David and Goliath. After that event, chapter 18 says that Saul took David into his service and did not allow him to return home, so he stayed to live in the King's palace. Saul's son, Jonathan, became such a close friend of David that the Bible says that he "had a close friendship with David and came to love him as himself," and from that time on they were like brothers.

The same chapter also says that everything that Saul asked of David, he did it so well that everyone respected him, including the soldiers and the officers. But David's success was so great that Saul began to envy him.

From then on, all the stories of David, Jonathan, and Saul are like a soap opera full of betrayal, death, forgiveness, crying, and pain, until chapter 31 of 1 Samuel ends with the tragic death of Saul and his sons, including Jonathan, whom David loved deeply.

Samuel was the last of Israel's judges, and he anointed the first and second kings of the Hebrews. The first king, Saul, lost God's favor by disobeying Him. Then the small boy who began to serve the king at a young age took his place and became one of the most powerful kings ever, with a heart according to God.

In 2 Samuel we are told all the stories about King David. Some are amazing, and some are not so good, because David made mistakes too. But unlike Saul, David had the right attitude toward God, and in his heart he wanted to please and serve Him. That is why God blessed him with the following promise, making an eternal covenant with David:

2 Samuel 7:12-16 "When your days are over and you rest with your ancestors, I will raise up your offspring to succeed you, your own flesh and blood, and I will establish his kingdom. He is the one who will build a house for my Name, and I will establish the throne of his kingdom forever. I will be his father, and he will be my son. When he does wrong, I will punish him with a rod wielded by men, with floggings inflicted by human hands. But my love will never be taken away from him, as I took it away from Saul, whom I removed from before you. Your house and your kingdom will endure forever before me; your throne will be established forever." And so it was, because from the descendants of David, Jesus was born, and his kingdom is everlasting.

Finish by thanking God for his love and mercy in spite of our sin, for seeing beyond our actions and believing in us, and giving us an eternal promise in Jesus.

Download the daily "Family" readings from www. e625.com/lessons.

The books of 1 and 2 Kings were named for their historical content of the most significant events from the time of the kings of Israel, other than those of the first two, King Saul and King David, which are told in 1 and 2 Samuel. These books cover the history of Israel from King Solomon, through the nation's division into Israel and Judah, until the dissolution of Judah under King Zedekiah. These books point out how idolatry and worship of other gods broke the people's covenant with God, causing the deportation and slavery of Israel and Judah. They ended up back where they started in the time of Moses, on the other side of the Jordan River and begging for a new opportunity. The author of these books keeps a record of these events to demonstrate to the captives that repentance from their idolatry is the only way to become a free nation again. Many of the stories in the books of Chronicles (chronicles of the kings) written by Ezra have the same purpose: to remind the people of Israel about their history so they can learn from their victories and failures, all to grow closer to God.

Welcome and introductory questions (10 minutes)

Before starting the lesson and after greeting your middle schoolers, take three minutes to ask three non-personal questions, designed to be inviting and unintimidating. These can be directed toward the whole class, or you can call on someone you know will be comfortable answering in front of the whole group:

If I were king…
    1- my first mandate would be…
    2- my first prohibition would be…
    3- I would like to be remembered as the king who…

All rulers try to leave a mark on history. Their dynasty is what makes them unique and special. Some have left a mark that no one can erase, even though for some we would prefer to be able to erase what they have done.

The first kings from the Bible are complex. Some were very popular among their people, others passed into history without glory, and others contributed to shaping the world as it exists today.

The king asks… (20 minutes)

You can do this activity as individuals, but it's best to integrate the group more and complete it as pairs. A quick way to form them is to have different paper shapes prepared in advance (circles, triangles, rectangles, stars, hearts, etc.) of different colors and sizes so that each shape is different from the rest. Cut them in half, put them in a bag, and ask the students to take one each. Then they simply have to find their identical other half. Note: you must place as many figures in the bag as there are students. If there's an odd number of students, you can let the last student choose which pair to join, or that student can be your helper.

You may have played this game a thousand times, but it's a good one because it makes clear the power of kings over their people. Before you get started with the activity, write on a whiteboard or poster board, or project with your computer, a list of things that participants must find. You can also simply use paper copies and hand them out to your students. Make a list of things that they can easily find around them (a green leaf, a black stone, the longest hair, etc., depending on where they are) and another with things that are more difficult to find or that require imagination (the shortest verse in the Bible, a live insect, the pastor's middle name, etc.).

Keep in mind that they only have 15 minutes for the activity. Use a bell, whistle, or something similar to let them know that time is up. Whoever has found the most things will be the winner (candy is a good reward for the winning team).

Stories of kings, kingdoms, and prophets (15 minutes)

While you are talking about the following characters, place their names on a wall or cardboard (or use a projector) so that they can keep in mind the sequence and relationship between the characters.

In 1 and 2 Kings we find the historical account of the people of Israel: fantastic real events, wars over power, betrayal, victory, nobility, wisdom, strength, deception, passion, everything! From the time of King David until the entire nation of Israel was taken captive, there were many kings who ruled. Some were successful, and some were failures. The most important and best-known of them are:

David: He was the first king after Saul and his life is in the books of 1 and 2 Samuel. The early chapters of 1 Kings begin with the transfer from David's reign to that of his son Solomon, and David's death.

Read 1 Kings 2:1-4.
What was David's advice to Solomon and why? Which promise did he bring up?

Solomon: He was the third king of Israel, the son of David and Bathsheba and the wisest man in history.

Read 1 Kings 3:7-14 and 4:29-34.
What did Solomon ask of God? What would you have asked for if you were in his place? What was God's request to Solomon? Did God keep His promise?

"But Solomon allowed himself to be seduced by his power and his amorous conquests; he turned his heart away from God and worshiped other gods, and the Lord withdrew his favor from him" (1 Kings 11:1-13). How did Solomon lose the throne? How did he offend God? What are things that distance us from God today?

Rehoboam, the son of Solomon, fourth king of Israel: This king listened to his young friends and, instead of helping the people, imposed more forced labor on them than before. The people revolted and no one was left to defend **Rehoboam**. Only the tribe of Judah did so, just as God had promised Solomon. All Israel except the tribe of Judah made Jeroboam king, and Rehoboam took refuge in Jerusalem with the families of Judah and Benjamin. That's how the kingdom of Israel was divided forever: on the one hand, Israel, and on the other hand, Judah.

Read 1 Kings 12:1-20.
How did Rehoboam fare for not listening to those who had experience, instead taking the advice of his peers? How did this argument that began with some routine decision-making come to an end? How do we react when our parents give us advice? Is it easier to do what adults say or what our friends say? Why?

Many kings in Israel and in Judea followed these three early kings. In the midst of so much chaos, God, who was always attentive and waiting for His people (who at times followed him and at times did not) sent some very special prophets to them, among whom we will point out:

Elijah: He never died, as he was taken to heaven alive. He performed many signs in the name of God. One of the most spectacular signs was that he prayed and fire fell from heaven, consuming an entire sacrifice (1 Kings 18:19-40). After several adventures, Elijah was taken to heaven alive (2 Kings 2:6-15).

Elisha: Elijah's successor. Elisha asked God for a double portion of the spirit that burned in Elijah, and God gave it to him (2 Kings 2:1-18).

Elijah and Elisha were prophets who honored God and that is why God decided to do great wonders through them. God presented himself to Elijah in a soft murmur and gave him the confidence and security to not be afraid, win the battle, and defend those who had never betrayed God with other gods. God could have shown how strong he was with an earth-shattering earthquake or an uncontrollable fire, but He decided to be the soft murmur, because His power is not in what is fearful but in His love and care for us.

Closing (5 minutes)

God always showed a special love for His people. He keeps all promises, the good ones and the not so good ones, too. Bad decisions cause us to suffer serious consequences, and to live apart from God is the worst decision. The rebellion of the kings led to God's people becoming divided forever, fighting among themselves, and having many conflicts throughout history. Solomon's disobedience had a consequence for everyone. Sometimes we don't realize that our decisions bring consequences for our entire lives, for our family or for our friends. If we depend on God, it will also help us to keep in mind the people around us and to focus on what is lasting and important.

Download the daily "Family" readings from www.e625.com/lessons.

Lesson 9 > JOB

The name "Job" in Hebrew means "persecuted" and in Arabic means "repentant." It's believed that the author of this book could have been Moses, because he had lived in the same city as Job, or perhaps Solomon, because of the style of the writing. From various descriptions in the book, it is believed that Job existed sometime between the story of the tower of Babel and the life of Abraham. The book of Job begins with the story of an argument between God and Satan, something that Job didn't know about.

Job's friends, and even Job himself in his ignorance, tried to explain Job's suffering from a rational point of view, until finally Job decided to trust only in his faith, in the goodness of God, and in the hope of redemption. God defends Job's trust by making this the central message of the book: When there are no rational or theological explanations for tragedy and pain, trust in God.

Welcome and introductory questions (5 minutes)

Before starting the lesson and after greeting your middle schoolers, take three minutes to ask three non-personal questions, designed to be inviting and unintimidating. These can be directed toward the whole class, or you can call on someone you know will be comfortable answering in front of the whole group:

1. If you had to choose to suffer one natural disaster, which one would you choose? Why?
2. If you had to choose to live with a physical disability for the rest of your life, which one would you choose and why?
3. If you had to choose to live without any one of the amenities that you have now, such as running water, electricity, or sewer (no bathroom in the house), which would you choose and why?

Often we take what we have for granted. For many of us, physical health, being able to walk or run is easy, going through a natural tragedy like an earthquake or a flood seems unlikely, and when we turn on the tap we expect clean water to come out without any problems. When bad things happen or things go wrong, it sometimes seems like the world is ending. It is only then that we realize how valuable the things we had were. Job's story is a tragic chain of misfortunes that befall him one after another. Perhaps by studying his story we can learn to feel a little better about ourselves and to be grateful even in our darkest moments.

Throughout the book of Job there are debates between Job and three of his friends, and after that a fourth friend intervenes. To better understand the book, we are going to divide into groups and discuss Job's situation.

Job's life (45 minutes: 8 minutes per station and 5 minutes to divide into groups)

Place five leaders in five different sections of the room. Give each of them one of the discussion points that follow. If you don't have enough leaders, ask four parents to help you for this class. If your group is not very large, ask them to help one station at a time. They can do it creatively, from memory, using decorated cardboard, a projection, or any way that's helpful, and ask the questions below. (You don't have much time, so do it quickly and if there is not enough time then skip some questions.)

You will need some preparation from the people helping you, but it will be a lot of fun if they are creative. Let students divide into each station with a leader as they wish. Leaders should start when you tell them to. Let students know when it is time to rotate stations.

Give a warning when four minutes have passed and only one minute remains to help groups manage their time. Point four is the most challenging, but the verses are there to guide the leader. That leader can choose one verse or paraphrase them. Look for people who have different talents for each group.

Station 1:
The debate between God and Satan: Job 1:1-12.
>   What do the first few verses say about Job and his family?
>   What things does God highlight about Job?
>   How does Satan justify Job's behavior?
>   Do you think God was right to test Job's faithfulness?

Station 2:
The misfortunes of Job, 1:13-22.
>   Job lost everything he had. If Job's story were set today, what things would he have lost?
>   What was Job's reaction?

Station 3:
Job's second test, 2:1-10
>   How does Satan test Job now?
>   How does Job's wife react?
>   How does Job react?

Station 4:
Job's friends: choose one of the verses or you can say them with your own words.
    Friend #1: Eliphaz: 4:7-9; 15:1-6; 22:22-30.
    What did his friend Eliphaz accuse him of? He believed that Job suffered because he had sinned.
    Friend #2: Bildad: 8:4-6; 18:5-12, 21; 25:4-6.
    What did Job's friend Bildad accuse him of? He believed that Job suffered because he did not recognize his sin or ask for forgiveness.
    Friend #3: Zophar: 11:5-6; 20:23-29; 27:13-17.
    What did Job's friend Zophar accuse him of? He believed that Job had not suffered as much as he deserved for his sin.

Elihu's advice: 32:12; 33:8-19, 29-30; 34:10-12; 35:8; 36:15-16.
How did Job's friend Elihu treat him? He believed that God used suffering to form God's character.

Things to think about, without answering:
When someone has an illness or goes through something very difficult, is it because of God's punishment? Can sin lead us to suffering? Why did Job suffer? Does sin have consequences?

Have you ever gone through something very difficult and your friends were with you? How did you feel?

Have you ever gone through something very difficult and no one was with you? How did you feel?

Have you ever gone through something very difficult and someone blamed you for it? How did you feel?

How would you like your friends to treat you? Like Eliphaz, Bildad, and Zophar? Or like Elihu?

God's response (5 minutes)
Read 38:1-3; 40:1-7.
God asks Job many questions to show His greatness, and how small we humans are.

Closing (5 minutes)
We often think that people get what they deserve. We often even hope they do. But truthfully, we would not want to receive what we truly deserve. We all suffer at some point, but it is never a punishment for something that we did or didn't do.

Sometimes we suffer the consequences of other people's actions, and sometimes we suffer the consequences of our own bad decisions, and sometimes we don't know why we suffer, but we must have assurance that God knows every sad moment in our lives. He knows everything that happens to us, everything that is missing, and everything that we need. None of our hard times is a punishment from God. Job wisely says:

Shall we accept good from God, and not trouble? (2:10, NIV).

God never promises that we will not have any suffering. We live in a broken world and suffering is everywhere. Many times we suffer because there are too many people who live in darkness, far from God, making selfish decisions, and we suffer the consequences.

Sometimes we need to get back on track (Acts 12:5-12). Sometimes we need to become stronger (2 Cor. 12:7-10).

In times of suffering, God always reveals his comfort and his grace (2 Cor. 1:2-7). Sometimes we don't know why we suffer, like Job. His friends tried to find the reason. God only brought out the best in Job. But God's faithfulness goes beyond all human perception and His desire for us is always good.

Finish reading: Job 42:12-16.

Download the daily "Family" readings from www.e625.com/lessons.

The Psalms are the ancient book of hymns of Israel, and the name of the book, both in Hebrew and Greek, shows that the psalms involve the use of rhythm or music. The Psalms, a book inspired by God (2 Tim. 3:16) define the spirit and content appropriate for worship. We can highlight at least seven authors of the Psalms, including King David, who wrote 75 of the 150 psalms, the sons of Korah, who wrote 10, and Asaph, who composed 12. Other authors were: Solomon (two), Moses (one), Herman (one), and Ethan (one). The other 48 psalms remain anonymous. The psalms were collected from the time of Moses until the post-exilic period, which covers about 900 years of Jewish history. In translation into different languages the meaning of the structure of this poetry and songs is sometimes lost. For example, Psalm 119 is structured acrostically: each of the 22 paragraphs, each eight verses long, begins with a word whose initial is a letter of the Hebrew alphabet, in order, using the whole alphabet. For the Jews, the Psalms were of great significance, helping them remember their history and beliefs in a simple and practical way. The Psalms present a wide range of theology applied to daily life events and, although they have not been grouped in thematic order, the topics cover the whole range of human experience.

Although the topics are too many to list, they are broadly classified as follows:

1. Wisdom Psalms: Instructions for wise living.
2. Lamentation Psalms: Meditations on the sorrow of life.
3. Kingship Psalms: Meditations on the sovereignty of God.
4. Penitence Psalms: Meditations on the consequence of sin.
5. Thanksgiving Psalms: Praise to God.

We will study this book by dividing it in two parts so that our students can understand the importance of this book in a practical and useful way:

1. **Praise:** strength, moments of joy, and exaltation of God.
2. **Fragility:** weakness, moments of fragility, and searching for the Lord.

This first lesson will be based on praise and the second will be based on fragility. Get ready to enjoy the creativity of your students, and be attentive to the needs and fragility that you will find in them.

Welcome and introductory questions (5 minutes)

Before starting the lesson and after greeting your middle schoolers, take three minutes to ask three non-personal questions, designed to be inviting and unintimidating. These can be directed toward the whole class, or you can call on someone you know will be comfortable answering in front of the whole group:

1. Who likes music, and who takes music lessons?
2. What type of music do you like the most? Who is your favorite artist, and why?
3. Which of the songs that we sing at our youth gatherings is your favorite? Why?

We all like to receive praise, nice words that fill us with pride for a job well done or for a task completed on time. How much more does God want and deserve praise! He is the Creator of everything! It's easy to say this, but if we stop to think about anything (nature, animals, a small seed, etc.) and the reason why it exists, or if we think about the human body, with each part fulfilling its specific function, or if we start thinking about the galaxy and the entire universe, we realize that we experience every day many miracles and wonders of God. King David knew how to notice this, and he knew how to express his gratitude to God in a very special way. In the book of Psalms we find many songs and poems that exalt God for His works and for His care.

War of songs (20 minutes)

For this game, divide the group into two: Make name tags or stickers in advance with two different images related to music (for example, a musical note and a guitar). Half the group should get the guitar, and half the group should get the music note. Give each student a name tag or sticker as they arrive, doing your best to make the teams even. Start the activity by flipping a coin to decide which team gets to start. This team must sing a song and then stop at any time it wants. The opposing team will have 20 seconds to start another song that begins with the letter or word that the previous team finished with.

Example:

Team 1 sings: "When the Spirit of the Lord comes upon my heart, I will dance like David danced. When the Spirit…"

Team 2 must begin with the word "Spirit" or with the letter "T," which is the last letter of the word "Spirit." So it could be: "Spirit of the living God, fall afresh on me…" Then the other team must start with "me" or "E," and so on. When one team cannot come up with a song to follow, they lose and the other team receives a point.

Play for 15 minutes. Students can choose to sing non-Christian songs as long as the lyrics aren't dirty or disrespectful.

Book review (5 minutes)

Music is, without a doubt, one of the main attractions in a teenager's world. Middle schoolers bond because they like the same music; they dress like their favorite band members, and even start friendships and relationships because they share the same musical taste. David would undoubtedly be a famous musician today, and would have recorded several albums.

The purpose of the psalms was to worship God, and reading them today inspires us to think about Him and what He has done for us. Singing psalms as modern songs helps us remember who God is.

Connections (15 minutes)

Give one of these grids to each of your students. There are two different sheets, to cover as many psalms as possible. Have students look for the verse in the Bible, find the phrase it corresponds to, connect it with an arrow, and finish it with a phrase of their own.

Download from www.e625.com/lessons the complimentary materials for this section.

My own praise psalm (10 minutes)

We talk to our Heavenly Father about many things. When we are sad, when we are happy, when a situation overwhelms us, etc. But let's be honest, most of the time it is because we are going through a situation in which we need Him. Many of us find it difficult to approach Him just to thank Him, to exalt His name, or to say beautiful things to God. Human beings go through so many feelings. Let's use some of them to express gratitude and contentment to God for feeling these beautiful things.

Give a piece of paper and a pencil to each student. Each one of them must write a psalm of praise. The challenge is that you can only praise God, not ask Him for anything. You can only thank God and tell Him how much He means to you, always in a spirit of praise. If anyone is willing to rap it, sing it, or recite it, give them the opportunity to do so for the group. Also, if they want to share their psalm privately with you or with another friend, offer them that possibility.

Closing (5 minutes)

God shows us through the book of Psalms His creativity, love, and joy, gifting us something as wonderful as poetry and music. We can also note that He loves it when His children come to Him with words of praise and gratitude. After all, our earthly songs and praises are a rehearsal for our glorious time in Heaven when we will praise Him face-to-face. Those beautiful words make God's heart happy, but He is even more happy when we worship Him with our lives. Let our songs of praise come from a heart full of real gratitude and of real actions that confirm what we say in song. God wants us to praise Him in spirit and in truth (John 4:23-24).

Download the daily "Family" readings from www.e625.com/lessons.

The Psalms of fragility reflect fear and anxiety. They are cries to God asking to be rescued. We will help students to look at their emotions and fears, and how we can cry out to God with the confidence and assurance that He hears us, protects us, and wants to bless us.

Welcome and introductory questions (10 minutes)

Before starting the lesson and after greeting your middle schoolers, take three minutes to ask three non-personal questions, designed to be inviting and unintimidating. These can be directed toward the whole class, or you can call on someone you know will be comfortable answering in front of the whole group:

1. What kind of things used to scare you when you were little?
2. What do you think is worse, being afraid of something or afraid of someone? Why?
3. When something is scary, what is the best way to get over it?

We all feel afraid at some point. Not all of us fear things that could jump out in the dark to scare us, and not everybody has a phobia of spiders or rats. But we may struggle with the fear of being rejected, or of failing subjects at school. Many middle schoolers are afraid of how others see them, or of what others say about them. Others are afraid that they may be seen as cowards or nerds, or that they are unattractive or simply losers. The Psalms can teach us about the inner fears that haunt us and weaken us.

The fears (10 minutes)

Write words on three large signs: Things, People, Feelings.

Ask students to place themselves next to, or in the area of, the category that they think adults are most afraid of.

Then ask them to place themselves in the area of what pre-teens their age fear most often. Explain that the "Things" sign also includes things like natural disasters, illnesses, accidents, and lack of material goods. "People" means that they are afraid of someone in particular, like a teacher who is strict, a parent, a relative who bothers them, or a bully. "Feelings" are loneliness, depression, pain, failure, anxiety, etc.

Now ask the students to return to the middle of the room. On a poster or white-board, or using a projector, make two lists:

1. Which of these fears can they control? How?
2. Which ones can't they control? Why?

Don't be afraid (20 minutes)

Give each of your students a copy of "Don't be afraid" and give them a few minutes to respond.

Download from www.e625.com/lessons the complimentary materials for this section.

Reflection on fears, anguish, and psalms of fragility (10 minutes)

As we saw in the book of Job, we often do not know why certain things happen. Other times, we may know that they are consequences of bad decisions, and/or the sin of people around us. We live in a broken world, and we need God's guidance to live well and enjoy life. But, like Israel, we turn away from God too often. People often prioritize doing what they want to do. Isaiah 53:6-7 is the prophecy of the cross of Jesus, and it says that we all abandoned Him, that each one of us went our own way. But even so, Jehovah bore on Him all of our sins. Christ suffered in silence, unjustly, feeling the pain of our abandonment and of bearing all the evil of the world. Jesus knows very well what it is like to feel sad and abandoned, what it is like to suffer the consequences of sin and evil. But unlike us, He did it to free us from pain, to rescue us and reconcile us again with our Heavenly Father.

As we saw in the previous class, the book of Psalms takes us into a world of poetry, enabling us to express ourselves to God in gratitude and praise. The Psalms also lead us to reflection, to pour out our hearts out before Him with repentance and sorrow for having failed Him, or with anguish over the situations we are facing. The psalms of David and those of other warriors are psalms of praise, of rescue in times of anguish, and even of praise in times of trouble. God is not afraid of hearing us asking Him: "Where are you? Why did you leave me?" Even Jesus asked Him that question. God wants you to seek Him when you are happy and also when you are sad. He wants you to rejoice in knowing that He will respond even when you are discouraged, because praising Him with confidence that He will respond at the right time will encourage you, lift your spirit, and give you hope and peace.

Closing (5 minutes)

Find one or two popular songs that speak about God's love and His faithfulness in times of distress and fear. If you have a band that can play live, or somebody who can sing with a guitar, that's even better. If not, find something online. (Make sure you have a good connection and audio loud enough to drown out any other noise.)

Invite your students to praise the Lord with their hearts, bringing to Him their sadness, pain and fears, but with thanksgiving, recognizing that He is faithful, and that His power can free them from all evil. Then close with a prayer. Offer to pray with those who want a prayer in private for a special situation. Tell them that they can raise their hand, and while everyone sings you can join one by one those who raise their hand and pray for them. It would be good if some leaders or parents can help you to pray so every student receives support in this way.

Download the daily "Family" readings from www. e625.com/lessons.

Lesson 12 › PROVERBS

The book of Proverbs, also known as the Proverbs of Solomon, is made up of the 513 most important proverbs of the more than 3,000 Solomon wrote. Proverbs is a book of comparisons between everyday images and life's deepest truths. Proverbs are simple illustrations that teach fundamental morality for everyday life, while reflecting theological themes as they apply to practical justice. The proverbs lead us to reflect, question our way of thinking, living, and managing our lives, in the light of truth. The two main themes in Proverbs are wisdom and folly.

Welcome and introductory questions (5 minutes)

Before starting the lesson and after greeting your middle schoolers, take three minutes to ask three non-personal questions, designed to be inviting and unintimidating. These can be directed toward the whole class, or you can call on someone you know will be comfortable answering in front of the whole group:

1. Who are the most important people in your life? Why?
2. Which of your secrets would you tell that person?
3. In which situations would you ask that person for advice? Why?

Many of us talk with our parents or other adults about things that we are embarrassed to talk about with our friends, and we talk with our friends about all the things that we don't think adults would understand. But the most important people are always those we trust with our secrets and to whom we go for advice. As we grow, we learn to be better sons and daughters, better grandchildren, better friends, etc., and little by little we also acquire the wisdom to be able to give advice to others.

Medicine for our relationships (20 minutes)

On a blackboard, a wall, or even on the floor, mark out the three categories of proverbs, and make sure everyone has the biblical quotes, but not the actual verses, in their squares. Print the verses on separate sheets.

Download the daily "Family" readings from www. e625.com/lessons.

Divide the group as follows: Before your students arrive, cut some paper in squares (or in any other shape), in three different colors and put one underneath each chair. Ask all your students to take a seat, and then have them look under their chair to see which color they got. Next they will form three teams by joining together with all those who got the same color. Each team will be assigned a different category, and will have a race. When the whistle blows, or at your command, students will have to look for the biblical quotes in the squares, find each verse in their papers, and place them where they belong. Whichever group completes the verse first will be the winner.

Divide the blackboard or a poster into three columns:

Complete table of answers for the leader.

Man's relationship with God	Man's relationship with himself	Man's relationship with others
Pr. 3:34 The Lord mocks proud mockers but shows favor to the humble and oppressed.	**Pr. 20:11** Even a child makes himself known by his acts, by whether his conduct is pure and upright.	**Pr. 17:17** A friend loves at all times, and a brother is born for adversity.
Pr. 28:13 Whoever conceals his transgressions will not prosper, but he who confesses and forsakes them will obtain mercy.	**Pr. 18:21** The tongue can bring death or life; those who love to talk will reap the consequences.	**Pr. 20:19** A gossip goes around telling secrets, so don't hang around with chatterers.
Pr. 6:23 For their command is a lamp and their instruction a light; their corrective discipline is the way to life.	**Pr. 3.3** Let love and faithfulness never leave you; bind them around your neck, write them on the tablet of your heart.	**Pr. 12:26** The righteous choose their friends carefully, but the way of the wicked leads them astray.
Pr. 10:22 The blessing of the LORD brings wealth, without painful toil for it.	**Pr. 29:11** A fool gives full vent to his spirit, but a wise man quietly holds it back.	**Pr. 18:24** A man of many companions may come to ruin, but there is a friend who sticks closer than a brother.
Pr. 17:3 The crucible is for silver, and the furnace is for gold, and the LORD tests hearts.	**Pr. 13:4** The soul of the lazy man desires, and has nothing; but the soul of the diligent shall be made rich.	**Pr. 16:28** A perverse person stirs up conflict, and a gossip separates close friends.

Is this too easy for your group? Then give them the list with only the names of the three categories, and all the biblical quotes, separate from the verses. Have them divide the verses by category according to their interpretation. The one who gets the most correct is the winner.

Important questions (10 minutes)

1. What are the verses in the first category about? Why do we say that they are about our relationship with God?
2. Why are we able to describe the verses in column 2 as giving us advice for ourselves? How do these help us to become better?
3. Why do we say that these proverbs are for interpersonal relationships? How does this advice help us with our relationships?

Emotips (15 minutes)

If you have at least three cell phones you can play this very entertaining game. Give a cell phone to each group, create a text message group, and copy popular sayings made with emoticons in your notes.

On the count of three, send the same sequence of emoticons to the three groups, and the first one to guess the saying is the winner. If you see that they have a hard time coming up with the answer, they can at least try to guess what it's about, even if it doesn't turn out perfectly. If you don't know one, replace it to make it easy and fun to play. You may need to adjust some words; use your imagination. You can also invent your own.

Proverbs have always been important because they are sayings full of wisdom that we can easily remember. All the proverbs from this book are excellent to memorize and to repeat every day. After all, they come from the wisest person in the world, of whom the Bible says: "I will give you a wise and discerning heart, so that there will never have been anyone like you, nor will there ever be" (1 Kings 3:12).

Closing (5 minutes)

Would you like to be so wise that people from all over the world would come to consult you? Would you like to have the secret of wisdom and intelligence?

The Bible has it: Read Proverbs 1:1-9 (NIV). What is it? (verse 7)

You will ask yourself: "The fear of the Lord?" Read Proverbs 2:1-11. The fear of the Lord does not mean that we need to be afraid of Him, but that we should have respect for Him and listen to Him, because we know He has the truth and the keys to wisdom and intelligence.

God is the source of all wisdom, and He gives us the key to obtain it. God wants us to be intelligent, to be able to think for ourselves, to choose well and thus live our lives to the fullest, maximizing our potential, without fear, at His side.

This is His final advice: read Proverbs 3:1-8.

Download the daily "Family" readings from www.e625.com/lessons.

Ecclesiastes

The title Ecclesiastes comes from the Greek word "ekklesia," which translates to "assembly" or "congregation." It refers to "he who calls or gathers," meaning to gather the people. In Hebrew, the name is "Qohelet," which literally translates to "he who collects wise sayings" or "he who addresses the assembly," hence the name "the preacher" or "the teacher." Along with Ruth, Song of Songs, Esther, and Lamentations, Ecclesiastes forms part of the Old Testament books called Megillot, meaning "five scrolls," which were read on five special occasions. Ecclesiastes was read at Pentecost. Its author was Solomon, probably written during his late years. The key word in this book is "vanity." The purpose of the book is to warn the new generations not to make the same mistakes that Solomon made. Being the wisest man in the world, Solomon wasted God's blessing so that he could obtain personal pleasure, instead of honoring the one who had blessed him with wisdom. Solomon went from glory to disgrace because of vanity. This word "vanity" is used 37 times in the book, emphasizing that earthly goals and ambitions are inconsequential. Solomon teaches us through his experience that the only way to find satisfaction is to live a life that recognizes God's sovereignty and serves Him. Solomon affirms that the highest good is found in obeying God and in fully enjoying life in Him.

Song of Songs

Song of Songs is translated in some versions as "The Song of Solomon," indicating that this song is the best among the 1,005 musical works of Solomon. Due to his skills as a writer and his ability as a musician, Solomon is said to be the author, but it is not known with certainty when he wrote it. The Jews would read this scroll at Easter, calling it "the holiest place." Far from speaking of lasciviousness, the ancient Song of Solomon exalts the purity of marital affection and romance.

The main themes in this book are God's love reflected in the love between man and woman and God's grace reflected in marriage. We can see how the book reflects God's character: God is faithful (8:5), God is loving (8:6), and God is pure (3:5; 4:1,16).

Welcome and introductory questions (5 minutes)

Before starting the lesson and after greeting your middle schoolers, take three minutes to ask three non-personal questions, designed to be inviting and unintimidating.

These can be directed toward the whole class, or you can call on someone you know will be comfortable answering in front of the whole group:

1. What do you consider more important: money, people's love, or having a talent that makes you stand out? Why?
2. If you could become a genius in any subject, which one would it be? Why?
3. What would you do if you had access to all the money you could imagine?

All people want to be happy. Everyone wants to find happiness, and most people work hard to be happy. Some think that having lots of money will bring them happiness, others think that being very important or reaching unique achievements will make them happy; others think that having a big family, having many friends, being famous, or other social connections will make them happy. But the truth is that there are countless cases of people who have won the lottery and ended up much worse off than they were before they won it. Artists who seemed to have it all ended up taking their own lives either on purpose or by mistake by overdosing. Getting the things we want is not the way to find happiness; true happiness is about realizing that we need something else. This is what the books of Ecclesiastes and Song of Songs are about. The truly important things in life, the desires in our hearts, and the ability to achieve God's purpose in creating us, are what will lead us to happiness.

Ecclesiastes and Song of Solomon were written by King Solomon, the same King Solomon who wrote the book of Proverbs. You may recall from the previous lesson that King Solomon was the wisest man in the world and, according to the Bible, there will never be anyone like him. The book of Ecclesiastes is like an intimate diary where Solomon shares his deepest feelings. He has studied so much, he has achieved so many things, he has visited many places, but none of that makes him feel how he wants. He feels that nothing in this world has value or meaning unless it is enjoyed within the plan for which God created it.

Work of art with wisdom (25 minutes)

Divide your group into four small groups. You can divide them as follows: Put colored pencils in a bag, with an equal number of each color of pencil per color, adding up to the number of students you have. If you don't have colored pencils, you can do this with colored straws. Then, group students by color. If someone wants to switch to join their friend's group, especially if it's their first time, that's fine.

Give each team a piece of cardboard or a very long strip of white paper and several different drawing elements, like colored pencils, paints, brushes, crayons, markers, etc. (I know that sometimes it is difficult to have these supplies available, but there are often parents and sometimes schools willing to donate new or partly used supplies.)

Give your students one of the following cards (if there are too many students, you can repeat the themes of the cards, or you can make up new ones). Ask them to read what it says and make a work of art that represents it.

Download the daily "Family" readings from www.e625.com/lessons.

Then they will explain what they made to their group. Tell them that it doesn't need to be a single drawing, or a single concept. They can draw parts, they can draw it together, they can draw it separately, but they should try to represent as much as they can on that paper.

In some cases the concrete thought will be very strong and they will draw exactly what they read. In others they will be a little more creative with images that represent concepts. We are going to give them the chance to explore the possibilities and enrich each other with their creativity.

Card 1:
Read Ecclesiastes 1:16-2:11; 7:1-14
Think about the key words in this passage, talk with your classmates about ways they can express Solomon's message and the new value scale.

Card 2:
Read Ecclesiastes 1:16-2:11; 3:1-14
Think about the key words in this passage, and talk with your friends about the ways they can express Solomon's message and the appropriate timing for each thing.

Card 3:
Read Ecclesiastes 1:16-2:11; 4:4-12
Think about the key words in this passage, and talk with your classmates about ways they can express Solomon's message, and the importance of community and family.

Card 4:
Read Ecclesiastes 1:16-2:11; 8:12-9:10
Think about the key words in this passage, talk with your classmates about ways they can express Solomon's message, and the importance of enjoying life and putting an effort in doing things.

Ecclesiastes carries warnings from Solomon. Just as an older family member might, he warns us not to put our hearts and energies into things that pass away, that do not last, that lose their flavor, or that do not lead to anything better. Ecclesiastes teaches us that everything has its time, that nothing is worth worrying about, that hoarding without sharing offers no rewards, and that our character, or inner self, is more important than anything we can find on earth.

This book also leaves us with one of the best pieces of advice for young people: Read Ecclesiastes 11:9-12:8.

Why would someone who has been through it all and has experienced all the best pleasures recommend this to us?

Deep love (20 minutes)

In addition to the book of Ecclesiastes, Solomon wrote another work of art: poems about perfect love. Song of Songs describes a scene of passion between two lovers, before and after they get married. Solomon compares this love story with the love God has toward His church: a deep, true, pure love. God IS love and one of the ways to express love as a couple is romantic love, in which attraction and passion are key. God created romantic love, and He put all those feelings in us. God knows our feelings, and has established the right time and the right person for them. That is why it is important to first understand the new value scale Solomon teaches us in Ecclesiastes, to understand what's truly important in order for us to fully enjoy true, pure love, like God's love for us.

Compliments (10 minutes)

What (appropriate) street compliments do you know? The kinds of things strangers say when you're walking down the street? How do they make you feel?

Think of some street compliments that are popular in your city, and bring them up if your students don't remember or don't know any.

Divide the group into two, girls on one side and boys on the other.

Divide these passages among the girls, to read as a group:
Song of Songs 1:15; 2:14-15; 4:1-15; 6:2-4; 7:1-9

Divide the following verses among the boys:
Song of Songs 1:12-14; 2:3-6; 5:10-16; 7:10-13; 8:6-7

How are these love verses similar to or different from the compliments we hear today?
How does each of them make you feel?
Which part caught your attention the most, and why?

Closing (5 minutes)

The Bible teaches many things, and they all are relevant today. The Bible gives us tips on how to live a life that's full of love and passion. God wants us to the life He gave us to the fullest. God wants the best for us. His advice is good for those who listen to Him. He is our creator, He formed our body and our feelings, and He wants us to do well.

John 10:9-10 says:
"I am the gate; whoever enters through me will be saved. They will come in and go out, and find pasture. The thief comes only to steal and kill and destroy; I have come that they may have life, and have it to the full."

Jesus is the door that leads us to salvation. This is not only the salvation of our soul in eternity, but salvation from a mediocre life, from the wounds that come from not listening to His advice and guidance. Satan wants to destroy us. With his lies Satan wants to make us believe that there are better things that we can achieve on our own, without God, that we don't need to wait until we fall in love and find happiness. But the Lord came to rescue us from that life of death. He came to give us an abundant life!

May Solomon's advice be engraved in our hearts like a tattoo so that we can enjoy that abundant life.

Download the daily "Family" readings from www. e625.com/lessons.

Obadiah

Obadiah means "servant of Jehovah." Obadiah's prophecy alludes to the historical situation in which the Edomites allied themselves with the enemies of Israel and participated in the sacking of Jerusalem. In Genesis 25:19-27:41 we read the story of the twins Jacob and Esau. Jacob convinced Esau to trade his birthright (although they were twins, Esau had been born first) for a bowl of lentils. Jacob was left with the best blessing and inheritance from his father. Jacob was the father of the people of Israel, and Esau was the father of the people of Edom. Esau later forgave Jacob, but Edom was always at war with Israel. While God told Israel that he must never return evil for evil because Edom was also his family, Edom took advantage of every opportunity to ally itself with the enemies of Israel and plunder their cities. God was not pleased with this, and judgment fell on Edom. As Obadiah predicted in verses 10 and 18, the people of Edom disappeared from the face of the earth.

Joel

The prophet Joel focuses his message on Judea and Jerusalem. His name means "Jehovah is God." Although the prophet shows detailed knowledge of the temple and its uses, he was not a Levite; he came from the tribe of Reuben. Joel 3:4-6 and 3:19 refers to the same events that are described in the book of Obadiah. The prophet Joel compares the way the Israelites were suffering from an invasion of locusts to the image of an army, suggesting that it was a portent of "The day of the Lord," a coming period of God's wrath and judgment, the day in which God would reveal His character. Joel calls everyone to repentance, promising that if they are faithful their land will be restored. The attitude of a man's heart and life before the Lord will determine his reaction on the day of judgment. Those who call on the name of the Lord will be saved.

Welcome and introductory questions (5 minutes)

Before starting the lesson and after greeting your middle schoolers, take three minutes to ask three non-personal questions, designed to be inviting and unintimidating. These can be directed toward the whole class, or you can call on someone you know will be comfortable answering in front of the whole group:

Download the daily "Family" readings from www. e625.com/lessons.

1. Which social injustices bother you the most? Poverty, slavery, exploitation of people...?
2. What kind of punishment would you give to someone who commits that injustice?
3. How would you compensate a victim of injustice?

The books that we are studying today deal with the prophecies from the prophets Joel and Obadiah, made on behalf of the Lord, regarding an injustice that took place. In the prophecies Joel and Obadiah share, the Lord becomes angry. He ceases to protect Israel because they have distanced themselves from Him. The prophecies also reveal when the Israelites turn back to God, He will punish those who are harming Israel. He will give them what they deserve.

I want them all! (20 minutes)

For this game you will need clothespins, at least three for each player.

Distribute the three clothespins to each player, and have students pin them to their sleeves. At the signal, everyone must try to steal as many clothespins as possible from other players. They must pin each clothespin they steal onto their own sleeves. They cannot hide them or keep them in their hands. Players can only use one hand; the other hand must be behind their back, and they cannot push players away or cover the clothespins. Set boundaries for the space players can use for this game. After three minutes, stop the game and see which player has the most pins. Don't worry if the game gets a little crazy, but you can stop it before the three minutes are up as needed. I suggest you play upbeat music for the duration of the game and turn it off when time is up.

Ask your students: How did they feel during all this craziness? Did anyone feel helpless? There was nothing they could do to prevent somebody from taking everything from them! Did anyone think the game wasn't fair? That the strongest, tallest and fastest players had a better chance of winning? Sometimes injustices hit us hard and make us feel despair or hopelessness.

Book review (10 minutes)

Prophets are individuals who communicate to God's people messages that came directly from God. In the Bible, most of the time these messages were not good news, but God's purpose in sharing these messages through the prophets was to restore His relationship with His people, to bring them peace and happiness.

The book of Joel compares the devastation the Israelites had suffered due to a plague of locusts to an army that would fall on Israel (ch. 1).

Joel then calls the people to return to the Lord, and tells them how terrible the devastation will be without Him (ch. 2). The Lord promises the Israelites much greater blessings when they turn back to Him with all their heart.

In chapter 3 Joel promises the people that when the day of restoration comes, the enemies who attacked and devastated them will be judged by the Lord; judgment will fall along with a divine promise that the nation of Israel will never again be invaded by foreigners.

In verses 4 to 6 of chapter 3, Joel talks about exactly the same events that the ENTIRE book of Obadiah is about. In Genesis 25:19-27:41 we read the story of the twins Jacob and Esau. Jacob traded Esau's birthright for a bowl of lentils (although they were twins, Esau had been born first). So, Jacob received the best blessing and inheritance from his father. Jacob became the father of the people of Israel, and Esau became the father of the people of Edom. Esau later forgave Jacob (Gen. 33), but Edom was always at war with Israel. While God told Israel that they must never return evil for evil because Edom was family, Edom took advantage of every opportunity to ally itself with the enemies of Israel and plunder their cities.

Joel 3:5 states, *"For you took my silver and my gold and carried off my finest treasures to your temples." God was not pleased with this and brought his judgment on Edom.*

Joel 3:19 says, *"But Egypt will be desolate, Edom a desert waste, because of violence done to the people of Judah, in whose land they shed innocent blood."* As Obadiah predicted in verses 10 and 18, the nation of Edom disappeared from the face of the earth.

In Joel 3:21 God says, *"Shall I leave their innocent blood unavenged? No, I will not. The LORD dwells in Zion!"* He unleashes His anger against Edom and other nations.

God did not simply abandon those who had suffered the devastation of the attack from those armies. In addition to giving those who had attacked them and robbed them what they deserved, He also rewarded and restored the victims of the attack and the people who were taken as slaves. He returned to them their lands and wealth. See Obadiah v. 19-21 and Joel 3:18.

The Lord pays attention to those who love Him from the heart, who surrender to Him and adopt Him as Lord. He wants to be our justice, He wants to be our refuge, and He wants to fill us with blessings. Loving Him means following Him, following Him means obeying Him, and obeying Him means paying attention to His teachings. He who loves does not harm but corrects in order to bless; that's how God wants to be with us. *"The LORD will roar from Zion and thunder from Jerusalem; the earth and the heavens will tremble.*

But the LORD will be a refuge for his people, a stronghold for the people of Israel. Then you will know that I, the LORD your God, dwell in Zion, my holy hill. Jerusalem will be holy; never again will foreigners invade her" (Joel 3:16-17).

Closing (10 minutes)

Give your middle schoolers a paper and pencil and give them time to write about a situation in which they were treated unfairly, or in which they were victims of something they could not control.

Focus on prayer, knowing that the Holy Spirit wants to act to cleanse the hearts of your students. Be prepared to have one-on-one conversations or pray with students who may want to do this.

Tell students that when your time together is over they can give what they wrote to a person they trust or to a leader, or they can tear it into a thousand pieces and throw it in the garbage. Remind them that God is just, that God loves them, that He will defend them just as He defended Israel. All they need to do is open their heart and follow Him.

Close with a prayer proclaiming God's love, His victory over injustice, and the blessings that the Lord wants to give them.

Download the daily "Family" readings from www.e625.com/lessons.

Amos

His name means "burden bearer." Amos was a fig gatherer. The prophet Amos, like Hosea (Hosea 1:1), was called to deliver his message to the northern tribes of Israel during a time of moral corruption. Amos speaks about two main themes: the absence of true worship of God, and the lack of justice. Like Hosea, Amos highlights the infidelity of the people of Israel. He presents a series of judgments from God against the nations, condemnation and then restoration. We will study the book of Amos but not Hosea.

Micah

His name is a play on words that means "Who is a God like you?" Micah was a prophet at the same time as Isaiah, and his message was also for Judah. While Isaiah prophesied in the castles because he had easy access to the king, Micah prophesied outside Jerusalem, on the border of Judah and Philistia, near Gath. Like the prophet Amos, Micah lived in a rural, agricultural area, far from politics and religion. Micah condemned social injustices and religious corruption, the same topics that Amos had spoken about to Israel some years before. When Samaria fell, thousands of refugees went to Judah, bringing their gods and rituals, causing a disintegration of moral values in individuals and society, something that Micah incisively addressed. In this lesson we will study how the prophet Amos addressed his message to the northern kingdom, Israel, and the prophet Micah addressed the same message to the southern region, the kingdom of Judah, a few years later.

Welcome and introductory questions (5 minutes)

Before starting the lesson and after greeting your middle schoolers, take three minutes to ask three non-personal questions, designed to be inviting and unintimidating. These can be directed toward the whole class, or you can call on someone you know will be comfortable answering in front of the whole group:

1. What is your favorite pastime when you are alone?
2. What things are only fun if they are done among many friends?
3. Have you ever done something you never thought you would do just because you were with a group of friends?

Many times we do things without thinking about the consequences when we hang out with the wrong people. It is not uncommon for a good person to get into trouble for not wanting to lose face with so-called friends who seem to enjoy doing evil or making fun of others. This topic is discussed in the Bible. Micah was prophesying against the inhabitants of Judea. God's people were mixing with others from neighboring nations, and adopting much of their behavior, spiritual rituals, and gods. God warns against all of this. Amos also warns the people for having distanced themselves from God, for having made false gods, and for loving evil.

A call with lots of interference (20 minutes)

Divide the group into two teams as follows: everyone must place their right shoe inside a large bag, box, or something similar. Mix them up as much as you can. The owners of the first shoes you take out (it will be half the group, depending on the number of players) will be one team, the rest of them will be the other team. Return all the shoes and do the following:

Place one participant from the first team at one end of the room (if the room is too small, go outside), and have the rest of the team at the other end. Do the same with the other team, but on the opposite ends. Give the player who is alone some headphones that will play music you pre-select, a pencil, and a piece of paper. Give the rest of the team a short message that they must shout to their player. The player who manages to copy the message most accurately will be the winner.

Rules: Teams cannot write the words for their player to read. Half of the team will try to make as much noise as possible to keep the player from the opposing team from hearing the message. The music should not be loud. If your group is large, you can skip the music part and make more than two teams. There should be no less than six players per team.

It was very difficult for the people to hear and understand the message of the prophets. The "noise" of society was too loud, and many people had become used to it. But the prophets did not remain silent. They had a clear and strong message from God.

Problems in Israel and Judah (15 minutes)

Have some of your students read the following verses aloud and then ask: What are the people's problems or sins? What does the prophet accuse them of?

> Amos 4:1
> Amos 5:10-12
> Micah 2:1-2
> Micah 3:9-11

Oppression of the helpless, mistreatment of the needy, injustice, lies, taxes, bribery, selling fewer goods but at a higher price, deceiving people, making evil plans, raising rents, violence, etc.

God's people, both in Israel and Judah, were going through difficult times. Both nations had distanced themselves from God, and as a consequence were doing horrible things against the most needy.

Sometimes when we get together with the wrong crowd we do things that we know we shouldn't. We commit injustices, we mock others or do evil, forgetting who we are and who our God is.

As we read the following list, have students write on a blank piece of paper a situation that comes to mind if. (As your students write, present this moment to the Lord and ask Him to clearly reveal to them what they have done due to peer pressure.) It may be that they offended someone, committed an act of vandalism such as stealing or destroying someone's property, or it could be watching pornography, horror, and violence, or consuming drugs, alcohol, tobacco, or other addictive substances.

Start reading this list while your students listen:

- If you have ever acted unjustly against someone, mocked their lesser status, mistreated a friend or brother, if you forgot who you are and offended the Lord, tell Him.
- If you have ever done something simply because your friends did it, because they watched, because they used, even though you knew it did not conform to your moral values, this is the moment to confess it.
- If you have ever stolen, destroyed on purpose something that belonged to others, if you cheated to make yourself look good to your friends, you can write it here.
- If you adopted a way of dressing, speaking, or behaving just because others did, and you know that it does not conform to your moral values and it dishonors God, you can surrender this to the Lord.
- If you have ever cut yourself, hurt yourself, or done something against your own body, you can confess it here, on this paper.
- If you have ever participated in inappropriate, sexual, or demonic games, if you have made oaths and promises that should only be made to God, you can write it here as a confession to the Lord.

Pregunta si alguien quiere compartir su experiencia, todos deben escuchar con respeto. Si así sucede, luego inmediatamente ora por tu alumno/a.

When they finish writing, tell them the following (10 minutes)

God knows all that we wrote on our papers. He knows everything, and we cannot escape from Him. He knows our feelings and knows why we made the choices we did. He does not punish us because of our mistakes, only out of love. God chooses to love us, and He waits for us to realize that we made a mistake, big or small. We all need to confess to Him because our "secrets" keep us apart from Him.

Micah 7:18 says: *"Who is a God like you, who pardons sin and forgives the transgression of the remnant of his inheritance? You do not stay angry forever but delight to show mercy."*

God's greatest pleasure is to love because He IS love. It's not that he HAS love and that because of what we do His love runs out. He always loves us because love is His essence: It is who He is.

Ask students to listen to the reading of the following two passages and then share their thoughts as a group:

Amos 5:14-15 *"Seek good, not evil, that you may live. Then the Lord God Almighty will be with you, just as you say he is. Hate evil, love good...".*

Micah 6:8 *"He has shown you, O mortal, what is good. And what does the Lord require of you? To act justly and to love mercy, and to walk humbly with your God."*

What was God asking of them, through the prophets?
- That they love to do good. Not to do it because it is the right thing to do, but because they love to do good.
- What does it mean to do good? Not to behave like good, boring children, but to have fun and truly connect with others!
- When and with whom? Whenever we can and with everyone that we can.
- What do these statements we are making mean in practice? How do they call us to change our attitude? (You can give some examples).
- Do we have to do good for God to love us? No, we saw that in Micah 7:18.
- Why does the prophet Amos say, "that you may live"? Because sin brings death and deadly consequences. Not only physical death, but also spiritual death: unhappiness, loneliness, frustration. See Psalm 41:1-2.
- Why does the prophet Amos say, "Only then will the LORD, Almighty God, truly be your helper"? (5:14). See Prov. 3:1-8 and 3:21-26.
- Micah tells us that the Lord has already stated what is expected of us. What is it? To act justly and to love mercy, and to walk humbly with our God.

- What is it like to act justly?
- What is it like to love mercy?
- What does it mean to walk humbly with our God? It means recognizing who God is and that we need Him, by asking for forgiveness for our faults.

If you want to, you can give your paper to someone, or if you prefer to tear it up, you can do so. We already know what God's promises are, that He forgives us because He loves us. We also know how we should act from now on, believing with certainty who He is and knowing how we should honor Him.

Download the daily "Family" readings from www. e625.com/lessons.

Isaiah was the prophet who ministered during the reign of four of Judah's monarchs: Uzziah, Jotham, Ahaz, and Hezekiah. Isaiah means "Jehovah is salvation." Isaiah belonged to an influential family with access to the king. He was raised in Jerusalem and had knowledge of politics and religion, which distinguished him from the other prophets.

Historically, Isaiah was compared to great thinkers, not only because of his message but because of the extraordinary way in which he wrote. He focused his message toward the southern kingdom of Judah. He condemned idolatry and, more than any other prophet, he also prophesied about hope and a better future. Isaiah provided information about Israel's future on earth. He is the prophet most mentioned in the New Testament, and his word is very powerful due to the large number of his fulfilled prophecies.

Also known as "the evangelical prophet," Isaiah spoke often about God's grace, especially in the last 27 chapters. Chapter 53 is a key chapter, in which he paints a portrait of Christ as the slain Lamb of God. In this lesson, we are going to highlight one of Isaiah's central themes, holiness, as seen in Isaiah chapter 6.

Welcome and introductory questions (5 minutes)

Before starting the lesson and after greeting your middle schoolers, take three minutes to ask three non-personal questions, designed to be inviting and unintimidating. These can be directed toward the whole class, or you can call on someone you know will be comfortable answering in front of the whole group:

Download the daily "Family" readings from www. e625.com/lessons.

1. Who is God for you?
2. In what ways do we serve the Lord?
3. Who are the people who know God the most?

Most of us have some preconceived ideas about who God is. We might all believe we are right, but God is not the same for everyone. We also limit ourselves to believing that service to the Lord means filling certain roles within the Church. Many of us believe that those who know the most about God are the people who teach or speak on His behalf. In the book of Isaiah there are many prophecies from God directed to various nations, not just Israel and Judah. These prophecies contain promises, condemnation, and restoration. In chapter 6, Isaiah shares about God in a new and amazing way.

Waiters race in the dark (20 minutes)

Divide the group into teams that each have four to six players. To divide the groups, get a sheet of labels of different colors. As the middle schoolers arrive, attach a small colored label to each player. When it's time for the game, ask them to group themselves according to their color. Within their groups, students should pair up with partners. One person in each pair will be blindfolded and the other will be the guide.

You will need to prepare a small area in advance. In this space arrange tables (the number of tables should correspond to the number of teams) with the same objects on each table: plastic cups and paper plates. Starting with the first pair, the blindfolded player must walk to the table, guided by their partner, who must stay in place and direct their partner using only verbal instructions. When the blindfolded player arrives at the table, they must recognize the elements by touch, then stack a plate and a cup and take them to table 2, all directed by their partner's voice. When the blindfolded player gets to the second table, they must place the stack on the table without letting it fall. The next blindfolded player must take that pile, add a plate and a cup to the pile and bring them to table 3 guided by their partner from point 2, which is the second table. At table 3, player 2 must leave the stack they were carrying in their hands and the third blindfolded player must place one more glass and one more plate and take it to the final table. This is done in a race between two or more teams. If you don't have too many players, the guide can be the same one for all four players. You can also use leaders or parents to make it more fun. If the pile falls off you must pick up everything, return to the table and try again.

When we're not able to see, even simple tasks become complicated. Most of us are so used to seeing everyday things that we take our sense of sight for granted. There is always more to learn and more to appreciate about the gifts we have received.

Main ideas (15 minutes)

We can see this in the book of Isaiah. Isaiah brought words of condemnation to kings and princes. He fought against hypocrisy, injustice, and oppression. By doing this, he was constantly risking his life. He knew what it was like to be unpopular; it was the consequence of communicating God's truth to powerful people. Isaiah knew God. He heard God's voice and obeyed it. But in chapter 6 we see that even Isaiah had a lot to learn. Even though Isaiah had served God many times, the Lord still had a lot to show him.

Read Isaiah 6:1-8 carefully. Even though Isaiah already was a prophet, it is not until chapter 6 that he truly discovered his calling. What can we highlight from reading this passage? Write the clues on a blackboard or another visible place:

1. **The Lord high and exalted:** In the original text it says YHVH. Isaiah uses this name in order to not pronounce the name of God, out of reverence. YHVH means "God is." Isaiah implies that he is seeing the one who is God, and is highlighting His greatness.
2. **The Seraphim:** They indicate purity, but even that is not enough for them to be able to see the glory of God. They cover themselves in God's presence.
3. **They sing:** "Holy, Holy, Holy" is sung three times, meaning infinitely holy. This holiness is so powerful that everything trembles, recognizing the infinite holiness of God.
4. **Isaiah is dying of fear.** He knows that in the Holy One's presence, he is nothing. Although Isaiah is a known prophet, the one who has the greatest number of fulfilled prophecies in the entire Bible, he is still impure in contrast with God.
5. **One of the seraphim flies to Isaiah and purifies his lips.** The seraphim declares Isaiah to be without sin; he makes him holy. Does this sound familiar to you? We are all saints because of the forgiveness of our sins. We have access to God's presence. But first we need to declare ourselves impure.
6. **"Who will I send?** Who will go for us?" Was Isaiah not already at the Lord's service? This question reminds us that many times we are satisfied with our role, and we believe that we are doing a good job. But we must be in communion with God to know His plans.
7. **Here I am, send me.**

Give each student a worksheet: "Between God and me," which you can download and print from the following link:

Download from www.e625.com/lessons the complimentary materials for this section

Conclusion (5 minutes)

God always has a better plan than our own. We often think we know Him and that there is nothing new under the sun. But when we find ourselves in His presence and He reveals Himself to us in His sublime essence and infinite holiness, we have no choice but to recognize who He is and who we are in comparison. God is God and He is infinitely holy. Before his holiness we are all sinners—whether we're a middle schooler or the most recognized prophet in the Bible, a pastor with a large Church or someone with very few friends. Until we recognize our condition before Him, He cannot sanctify us. God wants to make us holy not so that we behave well, not so that they think we are good people, but so that we can be in His presence and He can use us in powerful ways. That is why we need Jesus Christ. Jesus, through His death, cleanses and sanctifies us so we can have a relationship with the Father.

Sometimes we might feel afraid to think that God has a plan for us. Perhaps that is why He asks himself, "Who will I send?" But if we trust in His promises and in His majestic power, He will show us a future to which we will only be able to say, "Send me."

End the class with a prayer, recognizing that we need to be purified to enter into the presence of God so that He can communicate to us His plan for our lives and entrust us according to His will. Give thanks for everything, and ask that He can be revealed to your middle schoolers and work on their hearts.

Download the daily "Family" readings from www. e625.com/lessons.

Lesson 17 > NAHUM, ZEPHANIAH, HABAKKUK

The prophets are important not because of their individual characteristics, but because of their message. These three prophets all prophesy about the power of Assyria, which had its capital in the great city of Nineveh, the same city that one century earlier God had confronted through Jonah. Now Nineveh was once again full of people choosing to do evil. Their bloodthirsty armies laid waste to entire villages and piled up the bodies like mountains to display a spectacle of power.

Nahum

He was the first to predict the fall of Nineveh because of its evil. He said that the overflowing of the Tigris River would destroy the walls of Nineveh. He further prophesied about the city's demise (3:11), which later occurred after the Babylonian attack in 612 BC. The destruction was such that the remains of the city were not found until 1842 AD.

Zephaniah

He prophesied during the reign of King Josiah. After Assyria lost power and control of the region, Nineveh's rule weakened. For the first time in 50 years Judah tasted independence, at least for a time. Thanks to the influence of Zephaniah (who was of noble blood) and his prophecies, and thanks to having found the Book of the Law, King Josiah began to do good before God and brought great reforms to the government. It was during this king's rule that Zephaniah prophesied against various nations and peoples neighboring Judah. He also stated the fate that would befall Nineveh, just as Nahum and Habakkuk did.

Habakkuk

The book begins with a complaint to God for taking too much time to avenge the unjust violence of the Assyrians. God gives Habakkuk a vision, and tells him to write in detail the end in store for Nineveh due to its sins and bloodthirsty behavior. Habakkuk's prophecy includes the Babylonian attack to destroy Nineveh.
suerte que le correrá a Nínive así como lo hizo Nahúm y Habacuc.

Welcome and introductory questions (5 minutes)

Before starting the lesson and after greeting your middle schoolers, take three minutes to ask three non-personal questions, designed to be inviting and unintimidating. These can be directed toward the whole class, or you can call on someone you know will be comfortable answering in front of the whole group:

Anyone can take advantage of their power and authority. This can happen in families, at school, or even in churches.

1. Have you ever experienced bullying from someone older or an adult? Share about it briefly.
2. How did it make you feel, not being able to defend yourself?
3. Have you taken revenge for that injustice? Did anyone defend you or did what happened come to light?

At some point in our lives, someone older may bully us, despise us, make us feel inferior, or commit a great injustice to us. Sometimes they are slightly older than us (an older sibling, someone from a higher grade at school, an older neighbor, a friend's older brother). Other times they are adults, a teacher, even a father.

In all three books of these prophets, the people of the Lord were mistreated. They were taxed, they were killed, they were enslaved. The Assyrians were their enemies. The Assyrians had their capital in the city of Nineveh, and they were bloodthirsty and cruel. Not only did they kill all the people who opposed them, but they boasted of their cruelty and mutilated their enemies, making piles of their destroyed bodies and body parts.

The Assyrians were bloodthirsty, and they enjoyed being that way. The God we know would not allow things to remain like this. We will soon see how those who mistreat God's people will end up.

Activity (20 minutes)

We will do the typical tug of war, where two teams compete and the strongest wins. You will need a thick rope, colored tape in the middle of the rope, and colored tape to mark three stripes on the floor: the midpoint where the cinching will begin and two marks three feet from the central tape toward the ends. Each team should stand at one end of the rope, and at the signal they'll begin to pull. The team that gets the three-foot mark to cross to its side is the winner.

Divide the teams unfairly as follows:

First Tug.
Girls on one side, boys on the other. If there are not many boys, the leaders can be part of the team. We want to visibly demonstrate how unfair the battle will be.

Second Tug.
Place students in one row from largest to smallest, and divide them into two groups, the tallest and largest kids against the smallest kids.

Third Tug.
The leaders against the students, the same amount on each side. You can ask for the help of several parents who are willing to outright win a fight against their children.

Once finished, ask:
How did they feel about losing?
If it had been a tournament with a thousand-dollar prize, what would they have done to make it fairer?
In this game, the person who made the rules and directed the competition mistreated the weaker players. Do you think that person would behave differently if they were close to one of the weaker players—maybe their parent? How might the leader behave differently in that case?

It's likely they would feel discouraged, angry at the obvious unfairness toward the disadvantaged, and frustrated, perhaps, at not being able to play the game with a chance at winning.

If the leader of the game cared about the weaker players and intervened for them, they'd likely feel differently.

This is what was happening to the people of Judah and these three prophets. They were experiencing the injustices of being dominated by someone bigger, someone who was stealing from them and killing them with pleasure. For many years the people of Judah had to watch the Assyrians get their way, growing more and more powerful.

But God does not let injustices pass, even if sometimes it seems like it takes Him a while to respond. The Lord knows our suffering and only wants us to trust in His mercy, and His punishment for those who mock His children.

Injustice vs. God (20 minutes)
Give your middle schoolers the worksheet and at least 10 minutes to complete it. After the time to answer is over, everyone can answer the questions by reading the verses. Be sensitive in the first question. If no one wishes to answer, be prepared to share a personal experience.

Download from www.e625.com/lessons the complimentary materials for this section

Closing (5 minutes)

The Lord wants to defend us. He knows all our sufferings, He knows when we experience injustice, and He is not going to let things remain as they are. Nahum 1:7 says, "The Lord is good, a refuge in times of trouble. He cares for those who trust in him." For that reason, it is important to always be compassionate with our brothers and sisters, because He is their Lord too, and is jealous of each of His children. No one mocks God, and therefore no one mocks us, because we are His children. He is our refuge and our protector if we trust in Him.

Download the daily "Family" readings from www.e625.com/lessons.

Ezekiel

Ezekiel's name means "God's fortress." At a very young age, Ezekiel received his call from God to prophesy. The message that he had to communicate to the people of Israel, captives in Babylon with him, was simple but terrible. His task was to warn of catastrophe and affirm that this was God's plan for His people due to their own rebellious attitude. The city of Jerusalem and the temple of Jehovah were going to be destroyed, but God was going to also forgive those who repented and kept His commandments.

Daniel

Daniel's name means "God is my judge." He was a young man after God's heart who faced pressures and terrible threats against his life and those of his friends. He always chose to follow God. Daniel lived as a captive Israelite in Babylon. God called Daniel to prophesy about the things God would do to His people after Jerusalem was destroyed due to the rebellious attitude of the Israelites. Thanks to his God-given abilities, Daniel served as an advisor to King Nebuchadnezzar. He was a contemporary of Ezekiel.

Welcome and introductory questions (5 minutes)

Before starting the lesson and after greeting your middle schoolers, take three minutes to ask three non-personal questions, designed to be inviting and unintimidating. These can be directed toward the whole class, or you can call on someone you know will be comfortable answering in front of the whole group:

1. Imagine this: You get to school and sit down in your first class. What is the worst thing a teacher could say right then?
2. What phrases do your parents or other adults repeat to you all the time?
3. What could someone say to you right as you woke up that would make you happy for the rest of the day?

Ezekiel and Daniel were both very young when God called them to be prophets. They lived during the same time and in the same place, and were taken into captivity by the king of Babylon along with many other Israelites. Both had important roles since they were responsible for communicating what God wanted: that the people would stop their rebellious behavior, repent, and know that God wanted the best for them. Each had a specific message: Ezekiel for the people, and Daniel for Nebuchadnezzar, king of Babylon.

Messages with feelings (15 minutes)

Make posters with messages that have to do with things that interest middle schoolers the most and things they like least. For this you need to know your group. The messages below can serve as examples. A volunteer will read the messages you come up with, and the group needs to agree on the score they will give each phrase (one point for the worst phrase, the one they do not want to hear, and five points for the best phrase, the one they do want to hear).

Here are some examples. You should come up with more phrases according to what you know about your students:

"Tomorrow you will have a test."
"Next week you are going on a trip to a fantastic place."
"A beautiful surprise awaits you this afternoon."
"Fasten your seat belt when traveling in a car."
"Pick up your clothes off the floor."
"Who wants ice cream?"
"Did you do your homework?"
"Well done, excellent job."
"We are going to visit your grandparents."

Questions for dialogue:
Why did you give that score?
What happens when we hear things we don't like?

Review of the books (15 minutes)

At that time the Israelites were stubborn and did things according to their own thoughts, as they saw fit, without consulting God or taking Him into account: They lived in continuous sin.

When God spoke to Ezekiel, he warned Ezekiel that the people were not going to want to listen to him because they were obstinate. God asked Ezekiel to speak to them anyway. It would then be up to the people to decide whether to listen to God's message (Ezekiel 2:1-9; 3:7-10).

God then spoke to Ezekiel again. He asked Ezekiel to speak to the people of Israel and ask them to turn from their evil behavior so that they could live, because he loved them deeply. If the Israelites continued to be stubborn in their thinking, they would surely die. God asked Ezekiel to speak to them so that they would repent and not die. God warned Ezekiel that the decision to repent or not to repent was up to the people, but that if Ezekiel did not communicate God's message, they would surely be lost.

Read Ezekiel 3:16-19
How do we react when we see someone do inappropriate things?
Is it easier to stay silent or speak God's truth?

Another young man who had to speak and did not remain silent was Daniel.

Daniel became an advisor to King Nebuchadnezzar, a position he obtained because God had given him the ability to interpret dreams. King Nebuchadnezzar had a dream and he did not understand its meaning, so it worried him greatly. He sought answers among his wise counselors, and none could interpret his dream. They rec-ommended that the king seek the advice of Daniel (Dan. 2:1-3).

Daniel believed in God and trusted Him. He knew that if he did not interpret the king's dream his life would be in danger. He asked God to give him the interpretation of the dream, and God did. God listened to Daniel and gave him the interpretation, and Daniel went to tell King Nebuchadnezzar. To understand the king's dream and its interpretation, let's read Daniel 2:36-49 together.

In Daniel 3 the king had a great statue made of his image so that everyone in Babylon would worship him. The only ones who did not worship the king's statue were Daniel and his friends, who were also wise and God-fearing. The king became angry and had them thrown into a large furnace to burn them. But God sent an angel to take care of them, and they came out alive! The king worshiped God! Daniel 3:19-28.

Daniel had the courage to talk to a king about the things God wanted to show him, and Daniel had the bravery to refuse to worship other gods, even at the risk of his life. Daniel and Ezekiel were both brave in the place where God put them to speak. Daniel spoke with three kings throughout his life about God and His plans. While Ezekiel lived, he made a point of speaking to the Jews so that they would repent and return to God.

What is stopping us from sharing Jesus with others? (5 minutes)

Write on a blackboard, or somewhere visible, the reasons your students share.

For example:
- I feel shy.
- I'm afraid of being rejected.
- I think it's not important that I share with them.
- I don't know how to talk to my friends, my family, etc.
- I think they will not be interested.

Tell your preteens about a personal situation in which you experienced any of the feelings mentioned above, and how you resolved it.

Also share about ways that they can talk about Jesus and His work on the cross.

Closing (5 minutes)

Christians have an important message to share with others: Jesus' message of love and salvation. God loved people so much that He sent His son, Jesus, to die for them so that all who believe in Him may have eternal life (John 3:16). This message is unique and powerful, and all people—friends, family, schoolmates, everyone!—need to hear it. When Christ is at the center of our lives, everything makes sense. We are going to have to affirm our convictions and say, like Daniel, "I am not going to defile myself." The Lord will support us as He supported Daniel and his friends.

It isn't always easy to talk about God, to share His love and the things He has taught us through his Word. Sometimes we're afraid of what other people will think of us, or that they will make fun of us. But God is with us when we need Him. We must have the faith and trust to be willing to give our own fears for the cause of Jesus. Didn't He give up his own life for you?

Matthew 5:14-16 reminds us that *"You are the light of the world. A town built on a hill cannot be hidden. Neither do people light a lamp and put it under a bowl. Instead they put it on its stand, and it gives light to everyone in the house. In the same way, let your light shine before others, that they may see your good deeds and glorify your Father in heaven."*

Pray for your students that God will give them what they need to spread their message. Encourage them to share Jesus with their friends this week, inviting them to come to church next time. Pray that they will be examples and share the Lord with their neighbors, co-workers, or family members. In the next gathering, have students share their experiences.

Send them off in prayer and blessings.

Download the daily "Family" readings from www. e625.com/lessons.

The books of Jeremiah and Lamentations are books of outcries to God over the misfortunes that had befallen God's people because they were not repenting for worshiping other idols or for dishonoring God. Joshua had prophesied many years earlier about the destruction of Jerusalem (Josh. 23:15-16) and Jeremiah was later mocked for predicting the same thing (Jer. 1-35). When judgment was fulfilled with King Nebuchadnezzar's capture of Judah and the exile of the Jews to Babylon, Jeremiah responded with great pain, sadness, and suffering.

Jeremiah

Jeremiah was a priest and a prophet, and is known as "the weeping prophet." He lived a life of great suffering, and compared Israel's suffering to his own. His message was primarily for Judah, although we occasionally see him prophesying against other nations. He left with a remnant of Jews who fled to Egypt and was taken captive to Babylon by King Jehoiachin, when the king invaded Egypt. Jeremiah's main themes are the judgment on Judah and the restoration of the future messianic kingdom.

Lamentations

It is believed that Jeremiah is this book's author due to some instances of parallel language with the book of Jeremiah, and the comparisons between Jeremiah 7:29 and 2 Chronicles 35:25, among others. Lamentations comes from the Greek word "eka," meaning "loud wailings." As its name suggests, the book contains lamentations that recall the suffering over the fall of Jerusalem under the power of Nebuchadnezzar. This book keeps the memory of past glories alive, and teaches how to face suffering.

Welcome and introductory questions (10 minutes)

Before starting the lesson and after greeting your middle schoolers, take three minutes to ask three non-personal questions, designed to be inviting and unintimidating. These can be directed toward the whole class, or you can call on someone you know will be comfortable answering in front of the whole group:

1. Have you ever felt very sad? What caused it?
2. Has a close friend gone through something very difficult that caused them to be sad for a long time?
3. What was the best way to get over the sadness?

Some things in life are difficult to go through: the loss of a loved one or a pet, moving to another city and leaving friends behind, when parents divorce—these are things that cause deep pain for a very long time. We see stories of deep pain in the two books we are going to study today. One is the book of Jeremiah, a priest and prophet who went through much pain and suffering. He wrote about the pain of the people of Israel who were under the rule of other kings and nations. They were slaves and suffered all kinds of pain, punishment, forced labor, hunger, and abuse from those who conquered them. The other book is called Lamentations and the author is believed to have been Jeremiah. It expresses this same pain in its pages.

The Bible was written a long time ago, but we can see from its pages that people have gone through difficult times since the beginning of human history. Today we will see how we can get through those painful moments, move forward, and rise up from deep sorrow into eternal joy.

I have a problem on my hands (15 minutes)

Tell your middle schoolers that they are going to play a game that requires the participation of some cheeky volunteers.

If most of them are shy, you may have to come to their aid with some chocolate bars. This will be a "Truth or Dare" type challenge game, but without the "truth" part. Some of the challenges will be simple and anyone will be able to do them, but others may require a little more courage. What we will assure you is that none of the challenges will be inappropriate.

Each of the players will draw one of the cards from the stack that you will have prepared. After reading what the card says out loud, students will be able to say one of two things. They can say "No problem!" and complete the challenge, or they can say "I have a problem on my hands," put the card back in the stack, and draw a new one. The catch is that they must do the second challenge no matter what, regardless of whether it is easier or more difficult than the first. You cannot go back to the previous card, and all those who complete their challenge will receive a chocolate bar.

Print the "I have a problem on my hands" page and cut out the squares to use as cards. After playing this game for 10 minutes, ask the following three questions:

Download from www.e625.com/lessons the complimentary materials for this section

1. Why is that the same thing might seem very difficult for some people while being no problem ?
2. What can make a situation become a problem?
3. Why do some people seem to have problems more often than others?

Big Problem/No Problem (15 minutes)

Post a sign on one side of the room that says, "Big Problem" and one on the other side of the room that says, "No Problem." Then tell your students that as they listen to the following phrases they should get up and go to the side of the room where the sign matches how they feel about each statement.

- You got a bad grade on an important test and you need to notify your parents.
- You got into a big fight with your best friend.
- You just found out that your parents are considering getting a divorce.
- You forgot to brush your teeth before leaving for school.
- The biggest bully in school targeted you and won't leave you alone.
- Your uncle, who is not a Christian, has asked you to explain to him what being a Christian is all about.
- You have to decide whether you'd rather go to an amusement park with some kids you don't know too well or hang out at the mall with a good friend.
- You just found out that your family can't send you to camp this year, and all your friends are going.
- You are starting to have some doubts about God and the church.
- You're not sure what outfit you're going to wear for your school picture.
- You just found out that what you ate this morning at school is making everyone sick.
- You have grown faster than everyone else, and everyone is making fun of you.
- You hurt your mom with a rude comment.
- You have an assignment due tomorrow, and you can't find it.
- The new album you were waiting for has come out but you don't have enough money to buy it.
- You just found out that you will be living with your grandmother, and you don't know for how long.
- You're in a hurry and can't find one of your shoes.
- Your father just got transferred to a new job, and you have to move in the middle of the school year.

We all have problems at some point; hard times are part of life. As we get older, our problems seem to become a little bigger in line with our rights and obligations. That's the way we start preparing for adulthood.

Problems and Hope (15 minutes)

1- Jeremiah begins by prophesying about the disaster that will come upon God's people if they don't repent from worshiping other gods and turn away from evil. Jeremiah has a problem on his hands. He has to give them the bad news as a warning. Jeremiah 7:1-11.

2- Not only is it a warning that they do not want to hear, but Jeremiah himself will also suffer the consequences of his warnings. The prophet has a big problem on his hands. Jeremiah 20:1-2; 37:13-16; 38:4-6.

3- Israel has a big problem on their hands, as they have distanced themselves from God and now are suffering the consequences of their bad decisions. As Jeremiah prophesied, Babylon was going to take Judah captive, and they would suffer as slaves, but they don't want to listen, and now it is too late. Read Lamentations, and let students choose verses that affirm what was just said.

4- The Lord always has a plan (Jeremiah 46:27-28; 50:4-7, 33-34). God will rebuild in the future everything that was left in ruins. He keeps His promises and always seeks the well-being of those He loves.

Conclusion and closure (5 minutes)

These two books contain many terrible happenings. There is unfaithfulness on the part of the people that brings God sorrow, and the consequences of sin. This fills Jeremiah with sadness. He suffers from prophesying what will happen, and from seeing the people of Israel suffer during their years of captivity, slavery, and abuse by Babylon. The book of Lamentations contains outcries, wailing, and suffering. This teaches us that it is acceptable to feel sad, to cry and mourn for what is lost, for what is not gained, or for what makes us suffer. It's all part of living and growing. What is not acceptable is to remain in that state. We suffer the consequences of our actions, but we also should learn from them. We become wiser, and we learn to live better. We learn to trust in the Lord, in His Word, and we understand why it is good to obey Him. Obedience is God's love language, and He is always close to those who seek Him and obey Him. Our hope is in His promises.

Romans 5:1-5 says, *"Therefore, since we have been justified through faith, we have peace with God through our Lord Jesus Christ, through whom we have gained access by faith into this grace in which we now stand. And we boast in the hope of the glory of God. Not only so, but we also glory in our sufferings, because we know that suffering produces perseverance; perseverance, character; and character, hope. And hope does not put us to shame, because God's love has been poured out into our hearts through the Holy Spirit, who has been given to us. "*

Romans 15:13 says, *"Now the God of hope fills you with all joy and peace in believing, that you may abound in hope, through the power of the Holy Ghost. May the God of hope fill you with all joy and peace in believing, so that by the power of the Holy Spirit you may abound in hope."*

Close in prayer, asking your students what they want to ask the Holy Spirit for. Pray that the Holy Spirit will guide all of you to find comfort, hope, and the wisdom to make intelligent and mature decisions that will lead to fullness in Jesus.

Download the daily "Family" readings from www.e625.com/lessons.

After the Israelites spent 70 years of captivity in Babylon, in the year 538 BC, as a result of the proclamation of Cyrus of Persia, a first group was allowed to return to Jerusalem under the command and leadership of Zerubbabel and the high priest Joshua (Es. 1:1-4). Upon reaching the holy city they began to rebuild the temple that had been left in ruins. Due to the continued oppression of their neighbors and the indifference of the Jews themselves, the work was abandoned. That's when Haggai and Zechariah took action. They were sent by God to encourage the people to rebuild the temple and reorder their own spiritual priorities. Although they worked as a team, Haggai's message was focused on rebuilding the temple and rebuking the people for their indifference, sin, and lack of faith in the Lord. Meanwhile, Zechariah, living up to his name, sought to encourage the people to build the temple, confident in the promise that one day the Messiah would come to live in it, and reminding them of the Lord's promises and covenant to restore and bless them. It is believed that chapters 9 to 14 were written at a later period in Zechariah's ministry, which ended during the reign of Xerxes, the king who made Esther queen of Persia.

Haggai

Haggai's name means "festive." He was probably born on a festive day. Haggai is the second shortest book in the Old Testament.

Zechariah

His name means "Jehovah remembers." Like Jeremiah and Ezekiel, Zechariah was also a priest (Neh. 12:12-16). He was a contemporary of Haggai and began prophesying two months after Haggai. He was also younger than Haggai (2:4).

Welcome and introductory questions (10 minutes)

Before starting the lesson and after greeting your middle schoolers, take three minutes to ask three non-personal questions, designed to be inviting and unintimidating. These can be directed toward the whole class, or you can call on someone you know will be comfortable answering in front of the whole group:

1. What things charge you with energy and make you feel very motivated and active?
2. What things or situations discourage you?
3. When was the last time you got angry, frustrated, or discouraged over something? What was it?

The people of Israel had been taken captive to Babylon 70 years earlier. Finally, a king of Persia named Cyrus allowed a first group of about 50,000 Jews to return to their city, Jerusalem. They were led by two leaders: Zerubbabel and Joshua. At first the people were happy, excited, and joyful at being allowed to go back to their own country. But when they arrived they found everything destroyed: God's temple, but also their houses and the entire city. They began to rebuild, it wasn't long before they stopped focusing on rebuilding the temple, God's house. Furthermore, the neighboring people began to cause problems for the Israelites, accusing them in front of the king, causing divisions among them, and threatening to attack them if they continued with the plan to rebuild their temple. With all of this happening, it didn't take long for the work to stop. The divisions, the disaster that was the city, and the lack of support discouraged everyone so much that they lost the joy of being able to rebuild the temple for the Lord and to worship Him there.

What is it and where is it? (15 minutes)

Divide your group into at least two teams. Read through the game and decide if you want to make more than two teams, or if you want to have students play individually.

Take pictures of the most popular places in your city, especially ones your middle schoolers love. It can be the favorite pizza place, the train station, the downtown, the ice cream parlor, etc. Take each photograph from an unusual perspective. For example, from inside a store looking toward a display case, a close-up of a poster inside the movie theater, a server who works at the pizza place, etc. Number the photos and place them on a table in the room, or text them to each player. Then give a paper and a pencil to each group or each player. The first team/player to correctly identify the place where each photograph was taken wins (instructions below).

To find out who won, let everyone take their time to guess the answers. As they finish, have them give you their answer sheets. Once everyone is finished, gather students and begin reading the answer sheets in the order they were given to you. If the first player/team turning in answers was correct, they win. If not, go to the second finisher and check their answers. Continue until a winner is found.

Everyone will be curious to see the photos. If you can't take photos at favorite places, try taking abstract pictures of students—like of someone's elbow, ear, eyebrow, etc. To win, they must correctly guess who each photo is of. If you cannot print the pictures or text them to all the students, you can put them on a screen and have everyone write down their guesses at the same time. Make sure that they know that they shouldn't shout the answers.

Returning to the story (15 minutes)

Arriving at their ancient city and finding everything in ruins must have been very difficult for the people of Israel. Some of them had been born in Babylon and had never seen the city before, only heard stories. Others were old and remembered their splendid temple. In addition to the devastation they faced, they were exhausted from the trip and hungry (remember, there were no fast food places). The people felt increasingly discouraged. For this reason, the Lord sent a team of cheerleading professionals: Haggai and Zechariah, two prophets who gave them good news from the Lord to encourage the leaders and the people to complete their plan and rejoice over the promises that were coming in the not-too-distant future.

Have whoever identifies with the following raise their hand (10 minutes)

Then read the passages and let students respond by raising their hands:
Are any of you class clown? The family clown?
Are any of you always smiling, saying nice things to others, always in a good mood? Congratulations! These books of the Bible are about people like you.

- Read Haggai 1:2-4 and 11. What arguments did the Lord use to convince the people that they should build the temple?
- Read Haggai 1:12. How did the people and their leaders respond?
- Read Haggai 1:13-14. How did God respond?

When King Nebuchadnezzar destroyed the temple, not only did he take the people of Israel captive, but according to Ezekiel 8 to 11, when the temple was destroyed, the glory of God that dwelled in the temple also left. So for the prophets, rebuilding the temple was the way of inviting God to dwell again among them.

The cheerleaders (15 minutes)

Read the following verses. If you like, add also others you consider significant. Then ask students to try to put together a cheer (or a stadium chant) as if they were Haggai or Zechariah cheering on the people of Israel and their leaders.

Haggai 2:3-9
Zechariah 2:10-13
Zechariah 8:3 and 8:7-9
Zechariah 9:9

When they are done, take a few minutes to have students quickly share them with the whole group.

Closing (5 minutes)

Sometimes we feel as if we are walking on rubble. Sometimes everything seems to turn out worse than we expect, and our discouragement makes us lose sight of what is important. We forget the Lord by worrying about the problems we see before our eyes. But the Lord wants to restore His house so He can dwell among us with His living presence. In Him we find the answer to the worst of situations. He promises to always be with us, to give to us His Spirit, and to save us.

If we make sure to keep God's house standing in our hearts, He will take care of everything else.

Ask your students to write on a piece of paper about a situation that's bringing them down and making them feel sad. Then ask them to pass it to a partner they feel comfortable with, or to you. Whoever receives the paper should find words of comfort for their friend. Ask them to pray in groups of two or three for those situations. Students who don't dare share what they wrote with a friend can give it to you or another leader. Commit to praying throughout the week for the students who share with you

Close with a general prayer, asking for encouragement and joy from God in their hearts.

Download the daily "Family" readings from www. e625.com/lessons.

There are only two books in the Bible named after women: Ruth and Esther. Both are found in the Old Testament. We will now cover the second of them, Esther, to learn a little more about our wonderful God.

The book of Esther has a unique feature: Nowhere in the book will we find any mention of the word "God," But there is no doubt that God supernaturally intervened in everything that happened in the story. The book of Esther tells the story of a young woman, an orphan who was raised by an older cousin named Mordecai. God used her beauty to enable her to be chosen queen of a powerful nation, the Persians, in the place of Queen Vashti.

God's purpose was for Esther to save the Jewish people from an extermination plan orchestrated by Haman; Haman ends up receiving the punishment he deserves for his hatred of the Jewish people. Esther, under the guidance and advice of Mordecai, put into action the plans and purposes of a God who was attentive to both the smallest and most important details in the history of the Jewish people.

Welcome and introductory questions (10 minutes)

Before starting the lesson and after greeting your middle schoolers, take three minutes to ask three non-personal questions, designed to be inviting and unintimidating. These can be directed toward the whole class, or you can call on someone you know will be comfortable answering in front of the whole group:

1. Have you ever had to go through a time where you felt you needed to pray a lot? (An illness, a loss of a job or a home, etc.).
2. Who were the people who got close to you or to your family during that hard time? How did you feel about it?
3. Have you interceded for someone else who was going through a difficult time? How did you get involved, and how did you feel about it?

The book of Esther tells the story of a beautiful young woman who ends up being queen of Persia even though she is Jewish. King Ahasuerus (the father of King Artaxerxes, the king who allowed Nehemiah to go to Jerusalem to rebuild the wall) falls in love with Esther's beauty and charm. He names her queen in place of Queen Vashti (who, having refused to go to a party with the king, was removed as queen). God had a plan for Esther to become Israel's defender at a time when they were in danger.

Haman, one of the most important officials in Persia, hated Mordecai (who had raised Esther) because he stayed at the palace gates and, although there was a decree that everyone had to prostrate themselves before Haman, Mordecai would not do so. Haman swore to kill Mordecai—and not only not only him, but all Jews. Haman was ready to put his plan to annihilate the Jews into action. Queen Esther heard about Haman's plan, asked the people to fast and pray for her (she did so as well), and then she interceded with the king for her people, even though she was risking her life to do so.

In difficult times we can count on people around us who are willing to join us in crying out to God for our needs. It's an honor to be able to intercede for those who need our help in difficult times. God puts us in the right place to be there for each other in even the most complicated moments, including life and death situations.

The most beautiful queen (20 minutes)

For this game you will need plenty of newspaper and tape.
Divide your students into groups of no more than six. You can do it in the following way: place in a bag plastic rings (the kind sold at party stores) or any other type of jewelry, crowns, etc. Then tell students to separate themselves according to the color or type of what you brought.

Once divided into teams, give your middle schoolers 10 minutes to design an outfit for the queen. Each group must choose one team member to be queen. They should use the newspaper and other materials they got earlier to create a beautiful, regal outfit.

After time runs out, each group will present its queen. The team that designed the best outfit will be the winner. You can choose a few students or leaders to be the judges. While the teams work they can think about ways to assign points.

An amazing story of courage and purpose (20 minutes)

Have students stay in their teams to read Esther 3:5-11; 4:11 and 15-17; 7:1-6 and 9-10; and 8:16.

Materials: chalk, tape, creativity, and desire to play.

Draw a line on the floor with chalk or tape. The leader directing the game will ask questions about the story of Esther. One player per team must run to the line, step on it, and give the answer. Assign one or two linesmen to determine who steps on the line first. The player who gets there first will have the chance to respond. If the answer is correct, they get a point. If the answer is wrong, the player who came second will get a chance to answer.

1. Who was Mordecai? (Esther's cousin, the one who raised her.)
2. Who was Esther? (Mordecai's cousin, who became queen.)
3. Where was Esther from? (She was a Jew.)
4. Why were they in Susa? (Because they had been taken captive (this one is more difficult).)
5. Why was Haman so angry? (Because Mordecai would not bow down before him.)
6. What was Haman's plan? (To annihilate all the Jews.)
7. Why was the queen unable to talk to the king? (Because she couldn't see him without being called. Anyone who showed up to see the king without being called would get the death penalty.)
8. What kind of support did the queen ask from Mordecai? (To get all the Jewish people to fast for her.)
9. What did the queen ask the king at the banquet? (To save the lives of all the Jews.)
10. What was the end of Haman? (They hung him on the gallows he had built.)

If you have a tie, break the tie with a more complicated question, like what does verse 4:14 say? Let students look for it, read it, and respond.

Closing and conclusion (10 minutes)

In all of our lives, we will face difficult situations that will test our faith, our obedience, and our trust in the Lord. In these situations, it is important to have the support of the Church—other people who know and love God—to help us remain faithful to the Lord, no matter what we are going through.

We can count on the prayers, fasting, and spiritual support of our brothers and sisters in Christ, and they can count on us to do everything necessary to fulfill the purpose the Lord has entrusted to us.

The Lord is not mentioned in Esther's story, but Esther obviously trusted Him. That is why she asked her people to pray and fast with her. Esther understood that she was there to serve her people. When you go through difficulties, know that you can count on your friends and your faith family. The people you love and trust can support you in your pain and suffering. With the gifts and talents that the Lord gives to us, we can meet each other's needs and care for one another.

This is a good opportunity to spend time praying for those requests that are important to your students. Ask them to make a circle and join hands as you pray for one another.

So do not worry if they do not want to hold hands. Place leaders around the circle to fill in any gaps.

Prepare a box with papers and pencils so that students can share prayer requests there that they don't want to make public. Offer this after they have finished praying so that they can first have a time of sharing in trust and not all prayer requests remain private.

Additional technology resources: We suggest that teachers/leaders watch the movie *One Night with the King* by Gener8Xion Entertainment, director Michael O. Sajbel. If you think it will be appropriate and helpful, show a scene from the movie that demonstrates Esther's character, purposes, obedience, etc. to your group.

Download the daily "Family" readings from www. e625.com/lessons.

Both books, historically set around 400 BC, describe how the people of Judah returned to Jerusalem and rebuilt the temple and the city walls after the Babylonian exile, during which they had been slaves for more than 70 years. It took about 90 years from the time that the first group was released until the return of the majority of the people. Just as there were three deportations from Israel to Babylon, there were also three returns from Babylon to Jerusalem. The first was under the leadership of Zerubbabel (548 BC), the second under the leadership of Ezra (458 BC), and then the third was under Nehemiah, 13 years after Ezra. The book of Nehemiah is the last book of the Old Testament in chronological order, and the last record of God speaking to the people until, four hundred years later, an angel announced the birth of John the Baptist, who would prepare the way for the arrival of Jesus, the Messiah.

Ezra

His name means "Jehovah helps." He was a scribe and a student of the Word, strong and pious. He was in charge of rebuilding the temple in the city of Jerusalem. He was sent by the king because he had earned the king's trust due to his dedication, respect and knowledge of the word of God. His role as scribe is detailed in chapter 7:10: "For Ezra had devoted himself to the study and observance of the Law of the Lord, and to teaching its decrees and laws in Israel." Thus, he fulfilled his role to perfection.

Nehemiah

His name means "Jehovah comforts." Nehemiah was a man of action, cupbearer to the king, studious and disciplined, prepared to lead. When he learned that Jerusalem was in ruins and unprotected, he miraculously got the king of Babylon to not only give him permission to return to Jerusalem to rebuild the walls, but to also to provide him with everything necessary for building. Nehemiah even defended the people from their envious neighbors.

Welcome and introductory questions (5 minutes)

Before starting the lesson and after greeting your middle schoolers, take three minutes to ask three non-personal questions, designed to be inviting and unintimidating. These can be directed toward the whole class, or you can call on someone you know will be comfortable answering in front of the whole group:

1. Why do you think it is important to have a place where the church comes together to worship God and to learn his Word?
2. What other activities can be carried out inside a church? Try to think about social works, services to the community, etc.
3. What do you imagine the perfect church building to be like? What would you have in it that yours doesn't have?

During the Old Testament era, the temple was extremely important to the Jews, because that was where the presence of God dwelled. The temple was built and used according to many specifications. The temple priests fulfilled the role of interceding for the people before God. Very few people were allowed to enter the most holy place. If someone unclean entered, he would immediately fall dead. When Israel and Judah were taken captive, King Nebuchadnezzar took the most important things from the temple and destroyed it. God's presence was no longer there, and it caused the Jews to suffer extensively, not only because they had been taken into captivity but because they felt they'd lost their identity. They were without God, far from their lands, far from their inheritance, and once again living in land that belonged to other people.

Zerubbabel, Ezra, and Nehemiah returned to rebuild, little by little the temple, the altar, the walls, and the city. It was a difficult period but also a time of celebration, because God's promises to rebuild the temple and restore His people were fulfilled.

A delicate construction (15 minutes)

Divide the students into two teams, as follows: buy a deck (or more) of cards, put them face down so students don't see the cards, and have each student take a card. Those who take red cards will be the red team, and those who take black cards will be the black team.

One team will try to build a castle of cards, and the other team, without touching the cards, must try to knock them down by blowing on them. The difficulty is in that each member of each team will receive the same number of cards, and can only build with those. This way you can ensure that everyone participates, rather than just three or four students.

One team begins building. After two or three minutes (depending on how quickly they build), the other team can begin to blow from outside a perimeter you mark around the castle. After five minutes, have students stop. Count the number of floors that they've built and the number of cards still standing. Then the roles change. At the end of the next five minutes, the team that has the tallest building still standing will be the winner.

If you have students who don't want to play, you can use them as judges. If someone cheats, their team will be deducted one card each time.

The story (5 minutes)

God never tires of taking the initiative to seek out His people. This historical fact is the spark that lights the fire:

Ezra 1:2: *"This is what Cyrus king of Persia says: 'The LORD, the God of heaven, has given me all the kingdoms of the earth and he has appointed me to build a temple for him at Jerusalem in Judah.'"*

The king of Persia fulfilled God's promise from the books of Isaiah and Daniel.

Ezra 1:5: *"Then the family heads of Judah and Benjamin, and the priests and Levites—everyone whose heart God had moved—prepared to go up and build the house of the Lord in Jerusalem."*

The people wanted to rebuild the temple after having been slaves for 70 years.

Nehemiah 2:18: *"I also told them about the gracious hand of my God on me and what the king had said to me."*

Nehemiah encouraged the people to rebuild the wall.

In the books of Isaiah and Daniel, 140 years before Cyrus published his decree, God had anticipated that both reconstructions would occur. God Himself, prophesying through Isaiah, declared that He was the one who would give Cyrus his name, and who would put in the hearts of kings, prophets, and servants like Nehemiah the desire and the passion to achieve His promises. Wonderful God, eternal King... always fulfills His purposes.

The three constructions (30 minutes)

Give each student a copy of "The Three Constructions." As you go over the points that follow, give them time to reflect about themselves and give answers on their papers. Be sensitive to the answers. Ask the Holy Spirit to bring conviction and repentance to your mind and heart so that this class can be an instrument to draw everyone closer to the Lord.

Download the daily "Family" readings from www. e625.com/lessons.

Conclusion (5 minutes)

God's intention was to always remain with His people. His plan was to always dwell among them, to be worshiped by them, and to be their God, the one who protects them, blesses them, and gives them prosperity. But Israel was stubborn and screwed up over and over by doing what was offensive to God. The consequences for them were disastrous, and they ended up scattered throughout neighboring countries under the power of stronger rulers. God had His own plans, and He moved the hearts of those who were willing to serve Him so that they could return home and rebuild the temple, the walls, and, above all, their relationship with the Father. It doesn't matter what stage of life you are in. Perhaps you are just discovering the Lord and starting to understand what He wants for you; maybe you are at the point where you don't believe there is anything special for you in all of this; or perhaps you have already suffered the consequences of having distanced yourself from God. In any circumstance, God is always waiting to dwell in the temple of your heart. He is waiting for you to let Him come in to clean every corner and live there forever. Together you will build a wall so strong, so high, and so secure that it doesn't matter who comes to attack you or how they choose to do it. You will be victorious, and your inner city will be strong, healthy, large, and prosperous.

Close in prayer, thanking God for the reconstructions we can make through Him. May the Holy Spirit speak to the hearts of your students, healing any area in which they need help.

Prepare yourself in advance by praying to the Lord to give you a sensitive heart to detect any delicate situation, and to provide you with the words of effective counseling for those who need them.

We also advise you to look for counseling material in the three areas you are going to cover.

Download the daily "Family" readings from www. e625.com/lessons.

Malachi is a prophetic book. Malachi was a contemporary of Ezra and Nehemiah. His prophecy came after the Jewish people had rebuilt the city walls and the temple upon returning from slavery in Babylon. After Malachi, there were more than 400 years when God was silent.

Throughout the entire book, we can see evidence of the coldness and autonomy of the people in their relationship with God. God speaks tenderly to His people, and they respond with pride, full of excuses to justify their actions. The priests in particular were living a monotonous life, carrying out the sacrifices and teachings poorly and without any fear of God. God was displeased and offended and let them know: "Even in the nations that I have not chosen as my holy nation, my fame is respected and pure offerings are offered." God reveals the state of the people's hearts: "You say, 'It's too hard to serve the LORD,' and you turn up your noses at my commands. They despised the instructions that He had given them…" (Malachi 1:13).

Welcome and introductory questions (10 minutes)

Before starting the lesson and after greeting your middle schoolers, take three minutes to ask three non-personal questions, designed to be inviting and unintimidating. These can be directed toward the whole class, or you can call on someone you know will be comfortable answering in front of the whole group:

1. What are some of our routines when we gather here?
2. Why do we always repeat the same things in the meeting? Praise, prayer, announcements, sermon, offering, the Lord's Supper, etc.? What is the importance of each of these?
3. What could we do differently to make our time together more meaningful and significant?

Repetition and habit can make even meaningful things seem unimportant. This is what was happening to God's people during the time of Malachi. The worst had passed, and the routine of providing offerings to God and respecting His laws and commandments became less ceremonious for the people, and even for their priests.

Watch the following video: **https://www.youtube.com/watch?v=J9a_1xwM5Ro** You can look it up on the internet by searching: "The son never took his father as an inspiration." But the source and the producer are unknown.

The video shows a situation similar to how Jewish people lived under God's laws. They were simply not happy, they did not understand their Father, or why He acted the way He did. They could not enjoy their time with Him.

> Why doesn't the child understand what his father is doing?
> How does he feel when he sees his father doing all these things?
> When was he able to understand what his father was doing?

Main themes (15 minutes)

Distribute the following quotes (paraphrased), which were printed/written in advance on sheets of paper, and ask students to read them one after the other in numerical order, without pausing:

1. Mal.1:2: I have loved you, says the Lord. "And how have you loved us?" The people reply.
2. Mal.1:6: Where is the honor that I deserve? I ask you, priests, who dishonor my name. And then you ask me: "How have we dishonored your name?"
3. Mal. 2:17: You have tired the Lord with your words. And then you ask: "How have we tired you?"
4. Mal. 3:6: Return to me, and I will return to you, says the Lord Almighty. And you reply: "In what way do we have to return?"
5. Mal. 3:8: You have stolen from me! And you still ask: "How have we robbed you?"
6. Mal. 3:13: You attack me rudely. And then you ask: "When have we attacked you?"

- What is happening to God's people?
- Why can't they recognize that what they are doing is wrong?
- Do we ever celebrate the Lord, sing, pray, etc. without it really coming from the heart?
- Do we ever/often come up with excuses to miss/not be a part of/stop attending/not dedicate time to the things of the Lord? Have we said more than once "I'm tired" or "this doesn't make sense for me"?
- Do you think this is something people who don't know God notice when they join a Sunday service or a Bible study? Is it hard for them to notice our devotion and desire to worship God in everything we do?

Read Mal. 1:14. Have we given God what is left over instead of what is special? In what ways does this happen today? What does the Lord really deserve?

Read Mal. 1:12 and 3:14-15. Why were they tired of serving the Lord? Do you ever feel like your good behavior offers no rewards, and yet those who are disrespectful or greedy get their way? Do you think God sees the attitudes in our hearts?

Reasons to serve the Lord (15 minutes)

Ask your middle schoolers to give you reasons why serving the Lord is a privilege, and why obeying Him and offering Him the best of ourselves is the best thing that can happen to us. Do not limit the discussion to the service within the church. As they give examples, try to go beyond routine tasks related to church or youth group gatherings, and instead think about the roles of Christians in society.

As they come up with reasons, write them on a whiteboard or poster board, or project them with your computer so everyone can read the list.

Closing (5 minutes)

Without a doubt, God loves us and has always loved us (Mal 1:2). Someone who loves always seeks the good of the one he loves. How much more so God, the Almighty? He has always shown His people His goodness and faithfulness. Even when His people were unfaithful to Him again and again He always kept his promises (Mal. 2:5-6). Sin is not only doing bad things; it is also doing good things reluctantly or doing things not from the heart and then justifying yourself: "I always come to youth group," "I know all the songs," "I do all the hand motions," "I help in childcare"… If we bring before the Lord only our little bits of time, just going through the motions, we limit ourselves and we ignore how important it is to honor and obey the Lord. God seeks people who love Him as He loves us.

Read Malachi 4:1-5. Who does this promise speak of? Do we know and accept that promise? Why does our heart still stay the same? How can we worship Him from the heart?

Let us remember the reasons why it is good to serve our Lord. Finish by reading Malachi 3:16.

Close with a prayer of repentance, asking for forgiveness and understanding so you can worship God in Spirit and truth.

Download from www.e625.com/lessons the complimentary materials for this section

HOW DO THE OLD AND NEW TESTAMENT COMPLEMENT EACH OTHER?

As we've learned, the Bible is a collection of 66 books. This collection is divided into two large sections: one is called the Old Testament (OT), with 39 books, and the other is called the New Testament (NT), with 27 books. The NT books were all written in the first century after Christ.

A testament is a document that people will leave in writing to express their will. That is why we say that the Bible communicates to us the will of the Father. The Old Testament teaches us the will of God as revealed to God's people, the Israelites. In it are the five books of the Pentateuch that reveal the law by which the Jews were governed in ancient times (and some still are to this day), and the rest of the books are historical documents and prophecies inspired by God about the future. The New Testament begins with four Gospels that share many of the same stories; most importantly, the story of the birth, life, death, and resurrection of Jesus.

Jesus came to fulfill the law of the Old Testament and set all people free by paying the price for our sin, giving us direct access to God. In ancient times, only priests who had purified themselves could enter the presence of God. Now through Jesus all of us can be pure and can meet God personally. This was always God's intention. He wants us to be His children, loved by Him, the Father. This is so important to God that Jesus did not hesitate to sacrifice himself for us.

The OT is filled with God's promise about the Messiah, Jesus, who would set us free. In the NT the promise is fulfilled. The NT tells us about the three years during which Jesus ministered before dying, resurrecting, and returning to the right hand of the Father. The parts of the NT that follow are full of life teachings and doctrines that the disciples learned from Him and that were also revealed through the Holy Spirit. The OT helps us understand God's character. The NT shows us how we can get to know God personally.

The books of the Old Testament are divided into five sections and styles:
The Pentateuch (five books): Genesis, Exodus, Leviticus, Numbers, and Deuteronomy (the Law of Moses).
Historical books (12 books): Joshua, Judges, Ruth, 1 and 2 Samuel, 1 and 2 Kings, 1 and 2 Chronicles, Ezra, Nehemiah, and Esther.

Books of poetry or wisdom (five books): Job, Psalms, Proverbs, Ecclesiastes, and Song of Songs.
Books of the major prophets (called "major" because their writings are longer) (five books): Isaiah, Jeremiah, Lamentations, Ezekiel, and Daniel.
Books of the minor prophets (called "minor" because their writings are shorter) (12 books): Hosea, Joel, Amos, Obadiah, Jonah, Micah, Nahum, Habakkuk, Zephaniah, Haggai, Zechariah, and Malachi.
(Easy to memorize: 5/12/5/5/12).

The books of the New Testament are divided into four different sections:
The Gospels: Matthew, Mark, Luke, and John.
Historical book: Acts of the Apostles.
Epistles:
1- Paul's thirteen letters:
-Written during travels: Romans, 1 and 2 Corinthians, Galatians, 1 and 2 Thessalonians.
-Written from prison: Ephesians, Philippians, Colossians, and Philemon.
-Pastoral letters: 1 and 2 Timothy, Titus. (Some would also add Hebrews.)
2- General Epistles: James, 1 and 2 Peter, 1, 2 and 3 John, and Judas.
Prophetic book: Revelation (of John).

Welcome and introductory questions (5 minutes)

Before starting the lesson and after greeting your middle schoolers, take three minutes to ask three non-personal questions, designed to be inviting and unintimidating. These can be directed toward the whole class, or you can call on someone you know will be comfortable answering in front of the whole group:

1. Who likes to read? When you choose a book, what things attract you the most? (If no one likes to read you can ask them about movies or TV shows.)
2. If you were to write a book, what do you think it would be about?
3. If there were a book written about all the important things your family did since the beginning of your family tree, what part would you like to read? How it all started, the biggest challenges, the story of your most adventurous great-grandfather...?

The Bible is not one book, but a collection of books. Have you ever read a book series, or watched a movie with sequels? That is the Bible: a series of books that tell us the story of the beginning of all things. The Bible includes many historical events, action, violence, adventure, drama, betrayal, queens and kings, villains, visions, ghosts, monsters and demons, heroes and cowards—everything you can think of has already been written in the Bible. In today's class we are going to do an overview of the Bible.

National treasure (20 minutes)

Divide students into two groups (or more if necessary).

When they enter the room, have two boxes or plates prepared with two different but popular styles of chocolates or sweets, the same amount of each (approximately based on the number of students you are expecting. If you are not sure, just place a few of each kind and refill them only when both plates are finished—again with the same amount of sweets on each one). Each student can only choose one, and they can eat it, but they must keep the wrapper. When you are ready to play, divide them according to the candy they ate. If you need to form more teams, buy as many types of chocolates as the number of groups that you'll need.

This activity is a variation of a treasure hunt, except that as they find clues they will also find parts of the treasure. For this game you will need to create the clues depending on the place where you can play. Hide eight bags in different places, four bags for each team. Prepare four different clues with the locations for each team. For example, write "only women can enter" (for a clue to the ladies' bathroom) and hide the first bag behind a toilet, and so on. Give students their first clue. As they collect the rest of the clues, they can glue them in the spaces where they think they belong, or they can wait to do it at the end when they have found all four bags.

Note:

Try to get everyone in the group to participate. The more active players can go looking for the bags while the more passive can begin to place the pieces of paper on the skeleton. You can also shuffle the information to make it harder to locate the bags. Try to have one or two leaders per group to help organize students and make sure they don't disperse.

Give them a copy of the skeleton outline to complete, which you can download and print at the link below:

Download from www.e625.com/lessons the complimentary materials for this section

Prepare the following in Ziploc-type plastic bags:

Group 1: Each word is a piece of paper inside the designated bag.
Bag 1: The Bible - 66 books.
Bag 2: The Old Testament – 39 books.
Bag 3: Pentateuch - Historic - Poetic - Major Prophets - Minor Prophets.
Bag 4: All the books of the Old Testament, each on a separate slip of paper.

Group 2:
Bag 1: The Bible - 66 books.
Bag 2: The New Testament - 27 books.
Bag 3: Historic- Paul's Epistles- General Epistles- Prophetic.
Bag 4: All the books of the New Testament on separate slips of paper.

Explanation of how the OT and NT differ and complement each other (10 minutes)

When both teams have finished, using the skeletons they've completed, explain the differences between the OT and NT and how they complement each other, using the introduction to this lesson.

Use these new words to stick under each skeleton as you explain them:

Old Testament:
Law.
God in a limited relationship.
History of the beginnings of humanity.
Prophecy of a Messiah.

New Testament.
Fulfillment of the prophecies of the Messiah.
God in a close relationship (we now have free access).
Jesus and the new covenant.
History of the beginnings of the church.

Closing activity (10 minutes)

Prepare two bags with all the names of the books of the Bible, one bag and set of names for each team. Each team sends five participants to the front. At the signal, they each must draw a name, and arrange themselves in the correct order. The team completes this successfully first wins.

Note. Since there are only five participants, the books they draw will probably not be correlative, but they have to be arranged according to the order in which they appear in the Bible. Leave the charts they used previously visible so they can use them to guide themselves.

Do this three times, and the team with the most points wins.

It is important to know how the Bible is organized and where we can find each book in order to study the Word. This helps us to understand the importance of each part of the Bible and to visualize the progress of God's revelation throughout history. The Lord's Word is what guides us. It gives us strength through His promises, teaches us the truth, tells us about who God is, encourages us, gives us faith, and teaches us how to live according to the purposes of the God who created us.

To learn all these things, we need to read and study it. When we do, we will realize that even though the Bible was written thousands of years ago, we can still identify with it and learn from it today.

Download the daily "Family" readings from www.e625.com/lessons.

The word "gospel" derives from the Greek word "euangelion," which means "good news." The four Gospels are the good news about the most significant events in all of history: the birth, life, death on the cross, and resurrection of Jesus. The first three Gospels—Matthew, Mark, and Luke—are called "synoptic Gospels," because they share the same focus on Jesus' ministry in Galilee. The Gospel of John focuses on Jesus' ministry in Judea. The synoptics contain many parables, while John has none.

Although the synoptic Gospels are complementary, they also have unique points of view. Matthew speaks to a primarily Jewish audience. He presents Jesus as the long-awaited Messiah and the rightful King of Israel. Mark addresses a primarily Gentile audience, especially Romans, and presents Jesus as the servant who pays for the sins of many. Mark is thought of as the "action Gospel" due to the dynamism in the narrative. Luke speaks to a broader Gentile audience, especially to better-educated Greeks. Luke was a scholar and historian and presents Christ as the Son of Man who lived a perfect life to reconcile humanity to God. Luke is the only Gospel author who was not an eyewitness of Jesus Christ. He is also the author of the book of the Acts of the Apostles. John, the last Gospel to be written, was intended to strengthen believers as well as to present the Gospel to non-believers. He is also the author of the three epistles of John and of Revelation.

The four Gospels present us with a complete account of Jesus of Nazareth. God-man, fully human and fully God; the only sacrifice accepted by God for the forgiveness of the sins of those who accept His Lordship.

Welcome and introductory questions (10 minutes)

Before starting the lesson and after greeting your middle schoolers, take three minutes to ask three non-personal questions, designed to be inviting and unintimidating. These can be directed toward the whole class, or you can call on someone you know will be comfortable answering in front of the whole group:

1. If you could choose where to be born, where would it be?
2. If you could choose to be part of a famous family, which one would you choose? Why?
3. If you could choose between being born poor but becoming recognized as king by the people, or being born a rich king but not being loved by the people, which one would you choose? Why?

Throughout history, many people have been born in "golden cradles": being kings from the time they were born but without the authority or leadership abilities needed to govern. Today we are going to talk about someone who was a king from the time He was born, but had to earn recognition for His position. Although He was born King of all, He never occupied a royal throne on earth. That king is Jesus. We call him the King of Kings because He is above all governments. When Jesus walked the earth, the people did not want to recognize Him as the Messiah, and only a few knew who He really was. On one occasion, the Gospels say that "Jesus and his disciples went on to the villages around Caesarea Philippi. On the way he asked them, 'Who do people say I am?' They replied, 'Some say John the Baptist; others say Elijah; and still others, one of the prophets.' 'But what about you?' he asked. 'Who do you say I am?' Peter answered, 'You are the Messiah'" (Mark 8:27-29).

Those who knew who Jesus really was changed their lives and changed the world forever.

Activity: two in one (15 minutes)

Download and print the images of the elements you can view at the link below: a wine corkscrew that is also a bottle opener or a can opener that is also a bottle opener; an alarm clock that is also a cell phone charger; a computer that is also a tablet; a marker that is also an eraser; a wedding dress that transforms into an evening dress; sneakers that transform into skates; and other common things that have two uses.

Download from www.e625.com/lessons the complimentary materials for this section

You will also need a pencil and paper for everyone.
Place the images on a wall or a piece of cardboard, covered with paper to keep the students from seeing the images until it's time. Set a stopwatch at zero, and tell students that they will have 20 to 30 seconds (depending on the number of images that you got) to memorize what is in the pictures. Show students all of the images at once. At the end of the 20-30 seconds, cover the images again. Have students individually write as many things as they can remember in one minute. Once time is up, have students hand over their pencils. Uncover the pictures again. Whoever remembered the most images correctly is the winner.

Main point of the lesson (10 minutes)

Allow students to respond after each question.

What do these images have in common?

All images are objects that have two uses. Review the images and go over their different uses. Does the bottle opener stop being a bottle opener because it's being used as a can opener? Does the can opener stop being a can opener if it's being used as a bottle opener? No, it doesn't stop being what it is.

When Jesus came to earth He was like these elements that are two things in one. Jesus never stopped being God, but He was also fully man.

God wanted a relationship with people. He created us so that we would be His people and He would be our God (Gen. 17: 4-8).

Sin distanced us from God and made us NOT acceptable before Him. There were so many laws to fulfill in order to enter God's presence that no one was able to do it (from Exodus 35 to Deuteronomy).

But God did not allow things to fall apart. He had a plan to achieve His purpose of being our Father and having us be His children.

What was that plan?

Jesus. Prophets like Isaiah, Jeremiah, and Daniel began prophesying about Him hundreds of years before Jesus was born.

In order to save us, Jesus had to become one of us, be perfect, fulfill everything under the law, and thus be able to pay for our sins and reconcile us with the Father (Mt. 5:17-20).

That is why Jesus had to be 100% man, even though he never ceased being God (Mt. 11: 25-27).

Many of us are very familiar with the Christmas story

Who was the mother of Jesus? Mary.

Who was the earthly father of Jesus? Joseph.

Where was Jesus born? In Bethlehem.

Where did Jesus grow up? In Nazareth.

Was Jesus born knowing all things?

No, Jesus was a baby who needed to be breastfed, to have His diapers changed, and who cried at night. He had to learn to walk, He had to learn to talk, and His mother taught Him about the Law of Moses that all Jews learned. But Jesus always knew who He was and where He came from. He always had a close relationship with His heavenly Father, who revealed all things to him. Luke 2:52 says, "Jesus grew in wisdom and in stature and in favor with God and all the people."

Jesus was God, but when he became man he had to "grow" like all of us.

What do the Gospels tell us about the human Jesus? (10 minutes)

Prepare some slips of paper with Bible verses in advance and give them to the students. Give students time for them to look up the Bible verses , or prepare four Bibles with the verses already marked and pass them out.

The Bible says very little about Jesus as a child. Have someone read Luke 2:21-23.
During that time there was a man named Simeon who had been told by the Holy Spirit that he would not die without first seeing Christ. And verse 28 says, "Simeon took him in his arms and praised God." Jesus was a baby, so he couldn't decide what to do or where to go. Jesus' parents raised Him, and did with Him the best they could do.

Luke 2:41-43
Uh oh! Jesus was 12 years old...and he misbehaved! His parents came back for Him very worried.

Read v. 48
Why would they be so worried?

Read v. 49
Uhhh....Jesus argued with His parents? Does He sound familiar to you? Yeah...
He was 12 years old! Jesus knew very well who He was and who His Father was.
This section ends by saying that Jesus lived in obedience to His parents and continued to grow in wisdom and stature, like all other children.

Matthew 16:13-17
Nothing else is said about Jesus until He becomes more known at the age of 30 (Lk. 3:23). From then on He begins to declare who He is. Although He was God and defeated death (something no human was able to do or will be able to do), Jesus first lived as one of us. Jesus knows what it's like to live in this body made of flesh.

Jesus was 100% real.
Jesus was tempted (Mark 1:12).
Jesus became tired (John. 4.6).
Jesus got thirsty (John. 19.28).
Jesus got hungry (Mt. 4:2).
Jesus was distressed (Luke 23:44).
Jesus wept (John 11:35).
Jesus was betrayed (Mt. 26:15-16).
Jesus was abandoned by His friends (Mt. 26:56).
Jesus was mocked (Mt. 26:67).

But He was also God:
Mark 3:11.
Mark 9:2-4.
Luke 24:39.
John 1:31-34.

Closing (5 minutes)
Finish by reading John 18:33-37.

Jesus is the king of kings, awaited for centuries, the Savior, the Messiah. God among us. Immanuel (Is. 7:14), loved by His disciples and the thousands who followed Him, recognized as king by those who received Him, but crucified for the salvation of all. A king with a crown of thorns, who sat on a throne above all. Jesus, 100% God, 100% man. Jesus, who knows what we go through, what we suffer, what makes us happy, and what makes us sad. Because although He is God, He humbled Himself by becoming one of us. But He did not appear out of nowhere as a great king. He was first a child, then He reached adolescence, and when He became an adult He fulfilled his mission. Jesus did this because He wanted to get closer to us. He experienced in the flesh the things we experience today. That is why the cross was necessary: to give us life, to give meaning to the future and to our existence. Close in prayer asking for God to reveal Himself to your students.

Download the daily "Family" readings from www. e625.com/lessons.

In the previous lesson we saw the deity of Jesus, fully God and fully man, who suffered not only at the cross, but through all kinds of human difficulties and challenges.

As a child He was persecuted by Herod. As a teenager He struggled with His identity. As an adult He suffered rejection from people as He began His ministry. He also suffered abandonment by His friends, betrayal...and death on a cross. Today we will see who this Jesus was, the things He did and why He did them, and who Jesus is for us today.

We could do many lessons on the topic of Jesus' ministry alone, but today we will focus on the example Jesus' life on earth leaves for us. We will cover the Beatitudes, we will go through who His disciples were, and we will talk briefly about His miracles. If you consider it important to spend more time on any of these points, we suggest that you do this class in two parts.

Welcome and introductory questions (10 minutes)

Before starting the lesson and after greeting your middle schoolers, take three minutes to ask three non-personal questions, designed to be inviting and unintimidating. These can be directed toward the whole class, or you can call on someone you know will be comfortable answering in front of the whole group:

1. Who do you admire and why?
2. What would you like others to admire you for?
3. What does it take for someone to be admired?

Jesus led an ordinary life full of extraordinary acts. He was fully God and fully man. He had the patience to wait until He was 30 years old to reveal His true identity and fulfill His mission. Only 52 days of Jesus' life are recounted in the Bible, but they are 52 days that changed all of history. Jesus divided the history of humanity into two parts.

Who do they say I am? (15 minutes)

Jesus asks this interesting question several times of His disciples (Mark 8:27-29; Mt. 16:15, and Luke 9:18, 20) and of Pilate (John 18:33-34). But who is Jesus for us?

Divide your group into four smaller groups depending on where students are seated: just "draw" imaginary lines to divide them. If you only have a few students, specify who will do what. Designate one of the four Gospels to each group (or each student). Ask them to look through the Gospel they are assigned and share about the miracles of Jesus they read about there.

Write on a blackboard or poster board what they are saying. You will find the following:

Jesus heals.
Jesus feeds.
Jesus frees the demon-possessed.
Jesus walks on the waters/calms the storm.

All of those stories tell about the miracles Jesus performed during the days He walked here on earth.

Why do you think miracles were necessary?
What did these miracles say about Jesus?
What do these miracles mean for us today?
Have you ever experienced a miracle, or do you know someone who has experienced one? Share about it.

Jesus performed miracles because He was God, and He had compassion for sick and demon-possessed people. He wanted to set them free so they could enjoy their lives and so they could believe He was who He said He was. The miracles helped many to believe. Jesus taught people about faith, about the fulfillment of the Law, and about who He was. He also taught His disciples to act with faith, love, and mercy, and to give hope. In Mark 16:15:18, the resurrected Jesus tells His disciples what they need to do. We call this passage the "great commission." Jesus says the disciples are to go throughout the world telling the good news of salvation. In order for people to believe the signs that Jesus had done, the disciples would now also do similar signs through the Holy Spirit (Acts 1:8).

By the way…, Who were Jesus' disciples?
Write the disciples' names on a piece of cardboard. Leave this on display so students can memorize the names; you can talk more about the disciples some other time. Mark 3:13-19 is the most concise text on the matter.

Blessed (15 minutes)

Divide your group into smaller groups of no more than six people each:
As students arrive, give them each a drawing/printout of an emoticon or some popular cartoon or movie character. You can let them choose or you can assign

them, or you can instead put one image under each student's chair. Make sure the images are positive or funny, not offensive. If your group is very small, you can make one-person groups.

Prepare the Beatitudes from Matthew 5 on strips of paper, writing each of the phrases separately. Also write each beatitude correctly on a cardboard or blackboard to show students later. Keep this covered for now.

Divide all the phrases starting with "blessed" on one side and those starting with "because" on the other side, all mixed together. At the signal, the teams must try to correctly place each phrase with its match. They can't use the Bible; they have to try to make correct pairs on their own. You can do this several ways. Groups can work among themselves, organizing the verses on a table or the floor, or you can do this activity as a relay race where each participant in the team runs one at a time and sticks the verses on a wall with tape.

Blessed are the poor in spirit,
because the kingdom of heaven belongs to them
Blessed are those who cry,
because they will be comforted.
Blessed are the humble,
because they will receive the land as an inheritance.
Blessed are those who hunger and thirst for justice,
because they will be satisfied.
Blessed are the compassionate,
because they will be treated with compassion.
Blessed are the pure in heart,
because they will see God.
Blessed are those who work for peace,
because they will be called children of God.
Blessed are those persecuted for the sake of justice,
because the kingdom of heaven belongs to them
Blessed will you be when people insult you, persecute you and raise all kinds of slander against you because of me,
because a great reward awaits you in heaven.

Matthew 5:3-12

When you finish, see who has paired the most sentences correctly. Uncover the blackboard or cardboard that you prepared earlier and check students' answers against the actual verses. You can give the winning team a prize. We always suggest some sweets.

Then ask:
What does it mean to be blessed?
Which of all these "blessed ones" catches your attention the most and why?
How does what Jesus says compare with what the world tells us?

Closing and reflection (10 minutes)

Jesus came to teach us the truths of the kingdom of God, which are not the same as the world's truths: They are principles that give us life. He said, "The thief [meaning Satan, the prince of this world, Jn. 12:30] comes only to steal and kill and destroy; I have come that they may have life, and have it to the full" (John 10:10).
The world offers us many things that make us fall, make us fail, or leave us miserable (selfishness, vainglory, power—all the things people chase), but Jesus said: *"I have come into the world as a light, so that no one who believes in me should stay in darkness"* (John 12:46).

It's not surprising that the verses that follow the beatitudes, or "blessings," say: *"You are the salt of the earth. But if the salt loses its saltiness, how can it be made salty again? It is no longer good for anything, except to be thrown out and trampled underfoot. You are the light of the world. A town built on a hill cannot be hidden. Neither do people light a lamp and put it under a bowl. Instead they put it on its stand, and it gives light to everyone in the house. In the same way, let your light shine before others, that they may see your good deeds and glorify your Father in heaven"* (Matthew 5:13-16).

Jesus says He is the light of the world and that we are as well. What does He mean by these comparisons? Jesus came into the world to die for us and thus give us eternal life, and not only for that, but to teach us to live that life from right now on. He wants us to abundantly enjoy the life He gives us. Do we have to wait until we die to enjoy life in Jesus? Of course not! But He does not want us to enjoy life only for ourselves, but to also to be like salt, which gives pleasure to the world, and light, which helps others see in the darkness.

He showed us the difference between living for ourselves and living to honor God. This does not mean we should live as prisoners of laws, but rather live as if we are free from death and sin. Jesus did not come to break or annul the laws but to give the laws another meaning, a value that comes from the heart. This enables us to know what it is like to live free from evil and in full for Jesus.

He said, *"Do not think that I have come to abolish the Law or the Prophets; I have not come to abolish them but to fulfill them....You have heard that it was said to the people long ago, 'You shall not murder, and anyone who murders will be subject to judgment.' But I tell you that anyone who is angry with a brother or sister will be subject to judgment. Again, anyone who says to a brother or sister, 'Raca, 'is answerable to the court. And anyone who says, 'You fool!' will be in danger of the fire of hell…You have heard that it was said, 'Eye for eye, and tooth for tooth.' But I tell you, do not resist an evil person. If anyone slaps you on the right cheek, turn to them the other cheek also. And if anyone wants to sue you and take your shirt, hand over your coat as well. If anyone forces you to go one mile, go with them two miles. Give to the one who asks you, and do not turn away from the one who wants to borrow from you. You have heard that it was said, 'Love your neighbor and hate your enemy.' But I tell you, love your enemies and pray for those who persecute you, that you may be children of your Father in heaven. He causes his sun to rise on the evil and the good, and sends rain on the righteous and the unrighteous. If you love those who love you, what reward will you get? Are not even the tax collectors doing that? And if you greet only your own people, what are you doing more than others? Do not even pagans do that? Be perfect, therefore, as your heavenly Father is perfect (Matthew 5:17, 21-22, 38-48, NIV).*

Wow! What is Jesus saying? What is His message about?
Can we do any of this with our own strength? How can we achieve what Jesus is talking about?
Is there a way to be light and salt to others?
Do you want to walk as Jesus taught us?
What do you need to ask Him to change inside you?

Dedicate time for reflection and pray for your students, asking the Lord to give each of you His Spirit to be light, to be salt, to trust in the Lord, and live the way Jesus taught us, so we can be filled with abundant life.

Download the daily "Family" readings from www. e625.com/lessons.

In the first part of the lessons on the Gospels we learned about the deity of Jesus, fully God and fully man. In the second part we learned about His ministry on earth, His teachings, and His example. In this third part we will talk about the fulfillment of His purpose: His death and resurrection for the salvation of all who believe in Him. Get ready to rock your students' hearts with the most exciting story you've ever told. For today's class we suggest that you create a special environment so that they can experience with all their senses the great sacrifice that was Christ's death on the cross. Darken the windows with paper or fabrics that barely allow the light to pass through, or make small holes to make them look like stars. Look for dim lamps or candles (use battery-operated ones, or else pay close attention to the placement for safety—we don't want anything to catch fire). Flashlights or something similar will also work.

Dynamic

Make the largest cross you can, with two smaller ones placed on its sides. You can make them with paper and stick them to a wall, but keep them covered for a while so the students won't see them until later. Prepare a table on the floor using a piece of wood, an old door, a folding table—something that can represent the last supper. If you can have enough room for everyone to participate in the scene we'll lay out, that's great, but it's okay if you don't. We are setting up the last scenes of Jesus' story. Ideally, students and leaders should begin their gathering in a different space and then you can all go together to the place you've prepared. If your group is small, perhaps you can have them dress up so they can understand what is about to happen. Pre-plan the activity with adults who can help with the organization and the acting.

You could also prepare a play in advance, dramatizing the different scenes with the leaders and your students' parents, but if you do, keep it a surprise. (You can also improvise it with adult volunteers or with the students themselves.) Don't choose all men just because the disciples were men: choose from the whole group, so that everyone can experience Jesus' last moments up close. One student, leader, or adult, should be the "voice-over" who reads the parts of the story and then assigns the scripts. You can also use the Living Experience Bible.

Scene 1: (10 minutes)
The Lord's Supper
Invite the students to sit at the table (or enter the room where the table will be on the stage or in the room's center, and have the actors sit at the table with Jesus).

If you are able to prepare some snacks, such as chips, popcorn, peanuts, great. If your students are doing the acting, give them some of the parts they have to say, improvising on the spot as needed.

Matthew 26:20-30. Print several sheets with this part of the Gospel. At the end of dinner, sing a song of praise to the Lord, a cappella or with musicians. Singing the song is important because of what follows.

Once this scene is complete, pause the performance and ask a question for reflection.

1. How would you act if you knew one of your best friends, someone who shares your deepest secrets and knows you like no one else, is about to betray you?
2. The time had come. Jesus knew what He had to do. He knew what was coming, and He wanted to share it with His friends, because He knew He was going to suffer, and He felt anxious and afraid.

Scene 2: (10 minutes)
Gethsemane
When you finish singing, stand up and say, "Come on, join me." Have them walk a little, and let the next story begin.

Mark 11:26-36.
Once this scene is done, pause the performance and ask these questions for reflection.

1. Jesus needed His disciples to support Him in prayer so that He could pass His brutal test. Have your friends ever supported you during difficult times? Have you asked them to? How can your friends support you?
2. Jesus needed His friends, especially His three best friends: Peter, James, and John. Who are your best friends? Would they provide you with spiritual support during the most difficult moments in your life?

Jesus needed His friends, but even more he needed His Father for what was about to happen. Our earthly parents can be our best support when things are difficult, but our Heavenly Father is the One we need the most. When He helps us, approves us, and supports our decisions, we know the results will be for the best. Jesus was afraid. He knew what was about to happen. He was anxious and nervous. He knew His human self would suffer great pain, but His sovereignty would bring hope to the world. Have you ever experienced God in your pain?

Read or act out Mark 14:37-50.

Once this scene is done, pause the performance and ask these questions for reflection.

1. Jesus needed His friends, but they did not understand the seriousness and importance of what was about to happen to Jesus and they fell asleep. They were there, but since they were asleep they were unable to support Him in the way Jesus needed. Have your friends ever failed you? Have you ever found yourself in a situation where your friends were unable to understand you or support you as you needed?
2. Jesus had suffered a terrible betrayal. Now His friends, whom He had trusted, abandoned Him for fear of being killed. Have friends ever abandoned you? Do you know what it feels like to be left alone during a difficult time? Perhaps you have also abandoned a friend in need?

Scene 3 (10 minutes)
Jesus' Arrest and Death

In these scenes you will need volunteers to play the bad guys: the priests, Pilate, and the guards.

Read or act out Luke 22:54-71.

Once this scene is done, pause the performance and ask these questions for reflection.

1. Why did Peter deny Jesus? He was afraid. He had followed Jesus because he loved Jesus, but the situation became dangerous. Even though Peter was close to Jesus, he did not have the guts to identify himself as a good friend of Jesus.
2. Have you ever left a friend in a compromising situation and "got out" of the mess? Why? How did you feel after that? Did you feel like Peter did, perhaps?

First Jesus had to be judged by His own people, the Jews. He was judged by the high priest, the highest authority in their religion. The one who had taught the most about the Messiah and the hope in Him was now judging Him, and was unable to recognize Him. But even in His pain over this rejection, Jesus never lost sight of who He was or why He had to go through what He did.

Luke 23:1-2, 6, 11-21, 24-25, 32-33, and 44-46.

1. Finally, Jesus was put on trial by the Roman government. Although they were unable to find Him guilty of death, due to pressure from the Jewish people and the Jewish priests, it was decided that Jesus would be handed over "so that they could do with him whatever they wanted."

2. The religious leaders had finally achieved what they wanted: They got rid of Jesus, because He confronted them and pointed out their bad behavior. Correction is not always welcome. It is very difficult for us to accept when we do something wrong. Jesus did not come to change God's law and thus free us from feeling imperfect or sinful. He came to fulfill the law and perfect it, and in that way He was able to pay the price that we could not pay.

3. Jesus was dead, and all His followers were looking for answers. They were asking themselves, "Now what?" Often we ask ourselves the same thing: What do I do now with this Jesus that I know? But He has a plan for us.

Scene 4 (10 minutes)
Resurrection

John 20:1-3, 9-21, 30-31.

1. Jesus fulfilled His mission: He died, an innocent man, for the sin of all humanity, and was resurrected just as the prophets and He Himself had announced many times. Jesus always fulfills His promises and this was the most important one of all, because it marked a new beginning.

2. The curtain of the sanctuary was torn and through His sacrifice on the cross we all now have entry into the presence of God. Now we are clean and able to have a relationship with Him. We no longer need to make ourselves pure through our actions. We are purified through the blood of Jesus that cleanses us from all evil, so we can enjoy communion with God.

3. Jesus died, but hope is not in His death but in His resurrection. It is not in the grave but in the new life. He had to pass the most difficult of tests to win our soul. What is your response to Jesus' sacrifice? We all need the cross and we all need forgiveness. What are you going to offer Jesus today? He is only waiting for you to give Him your heart so that He can teach you how to live life in full.

Closing (5 minutes)
Close with a prayer of gratitude, a confession of sins and of repentance, giving your students time to confess. Finish by praying with joy for our salvation.

If you have time, have students write down the things they want to deliver on the cross to symbolize that Jesus already took them with Him when He was crucified.

Close your time together with a prayer confessing your faith.

Download the daily "Family" readings from www.e625.com/lessons.

Chapters 1-5: The Holy Spirit's arrival and the beginning of the apostles' ministry.

The book of the Acts of the apostles was written by Luke. As it says at the start, it is the second book addressed to Theophilus. The first book dedicated to Theophilus is the Gospel according to Luke. It is not known who Theophilus was, but we can assume from Luke's expression "oh distinguished [or "most excellent"] Theophilus" in Luke 1:3 that he was a person of influence and power. Acts includes the great stories of notable characters from the early days of the early church, primarily the acts of Peter and Paul. These events involved the direction, training, and ministry of the Holy Spirit, working through the apostles and their first disciples in forming the church and its influence in the world and history.

We are going to divide this book into three large sections, resulting in three lessons:
1. The beginning of the Church in Jerusalem. Acts 1-5
2. The Church in Palestine. Acts 6-12
3. The extension of the church to the rest of Asia Minor and Europe. Acts 13-28

These sections cover the ascension of Jesus, the arrival of the Holy Spirit, and the beginning of the ministry of the apostles.

Welcome and introductory questions (10 minutes)

Before starting the lesson and after greeting your middle schoolers, take three minutes to ask three non-personal questions, designed to be inviting and unintimidating. These can be directed toward the whole class, or you can call on someone you know will be comfortable answering in front of the whole group:

1. What talent do you have? What comes easily to you? What talent would you like to learn?
2. How could you develop it, improve it, or learn it?
3. If you could buy something that would enhance your talent 100%, what would it be?

Almost all of us would like to be able to stand out with our own unique talent. If we had an amazing talent, we would want to show it off at every opportunity. Maybe we'd even enter competitions and contests.

Luke begins the story in the book of Acts right where he ended his previous book, the Gospel according to Luke: with the resurrected Jesus. Until that moment, Jesus' disciples had followed Him like little ducklings following mother duck, learning from Him and sometimes practicing what they learned. But this is the moment when Jesus sends them on their own to continue with the mission. Actually, though, they were not on their own, because He literally sent them an "upgrade" that would help them and be with them. That is what we are going to learn about today.

Before and after (10 minutes)

Show students images of machines and gadgets: what they looked like before electricity, and how they were improved with electricity. You can download and print these images from the complimentary materials in the link below.

Download from www.e625.com/lessons the complimentary materials for this section

Jesus walked with His disciples, and He was their example, teaching them so that they could later also be teachers and leaders. He gave them faith and trained them to be the first leaders of the church of Jesus Christ. But, just as we probably were the first time we slept in a friend's house away from our own bed and our family, the disciples were scared, fearful, doubtful, and somewhat confused. Following Jesus had been difficult, and now they had to remember all the lessons and be strong and intelligent, just as their leader had been.

Jesus and the Father knew that the disciples needed supernatural help to guide them, remind them of what they had learned, and fill them with faith and abilities they did not even know they had. This superpower was God himself in His third person, the Holy Spirit. God was the creator of all things, Jesus was God made flesh, and the Holy Spirit was God within them, helping them to achieve the mission.

It's pretty much like being able to plug into something and downloading the latest update for a unique talent. The disciples already had the foundation, the example, and the inspiration. The Holy Spirit was the most powerful upgrade, the supercharge that would take them to their maximum potential, just like electricity did to the train or the washing machine. Without the power of the Holy Spirit perhaps they would have achieved some things, but it is very likely that they would have given up at the first difficulty. So it is with us too. God's Spirit is a promise given to all of us who believe in Jesus as our Savior (5:32). It is only through Him that we manage to live life to its maximum potential, focused on what matters, ready to face difficulties, and prepared to bring the message of salvation to those who do not yet have it.

Important readings (20 minutes

Divide the following verses among your students. You can mark them in a Bible in advance and have them pass it around, or you can write the verses on pieces of paper. You can also divide the students into groups to read the verses and answer the questions.

The promise: Acts 1:5-9
- What is the Holy Spirit?
- What does Jesus tell the disciples they need the Holy Spirit for?

The fulfillment: 2:1-4, 38-39
- How did they receive the Holy Spirit the first time?
- What does Peter recommend to the people who witnessed the Holy Spirit coming upon the believers?
- For whom is the promise of the Spirit?

The action: 3:1-10; 5:12-16
- What things were they able to accomplish afterward?

The cost: 4:1-5, 16-20, 29-31; 5:17-24, 28-32, 41-42
- Why were they arrested?
- How did Peter and John respond when others attempted to silence them?
- What happened when they prayed?

Closing (10 minutes)

Sharing the Lord with our friends is often not as easy as we would like it to be. But with the power of the Holy Spirit and by being faithful to the Lord we can achieve impossible things. Just as the apostles needed the Holy Spirit to accomplish what they needed to, we also need Him today. He can manifest Himself in many different ways, but His power is still the same. Without Him we cannot please God, because in our own strength we are like that old washing machine that requires lots of time and effort to wash the clothes, or that heavy steam train that moves forward, but only very slowly. With the Holy Spirit we can "plug in" to the Lord and we'll understand His message, live within His will, and bring His message to our friends and family.

But let's start from the inside out.

What are some things you currently find very difficult? How would you want the Lord to "supercharge" you with power to overcome a hard situation?
Is there anyone you know needs the Lord, but you haven't dared to tell them about Him? How can you show that person God's love without using words?

The Holy Spirit was promised by Jesus thousands of years ago, and the Holy Spirit remains a reality for all of us who love God and confess Him as Lord. We all need God's power to overcome our difficulties, to be faithful to Him, and to be His witnesses. Say a prayer of confession, giving time for your students to confess their difficulties to the Lord in prayer. Keep praying for repentance and surrender. And finally, ask the Lord to bless your students with his Spirit so that they can be His disciples, carrying out the Word of God with power.

Download the daily "Family" readings from www.e625.com/lessons.

Chapters 6-12: The church spreads throughout Palestine and to the Gentiles.

Welcome and introductory questions (10 minutes)

Before starting the lesson and after greeting your middle schoolers, take three minutes to ask three non-personal questions, designed to be inviting and unintimidating. These can be directed toward the whole class, or you can call on someone you know will be comfortable answering in front of the whole group:

1. Which are the types of suffering that we most often see or hear about from people?
2. If you could end one of them, which one would you choose and why?
3. Would you do it for free, or even spend your own money to achieve it?

Jesus' disciples had something wonderful to tell everyone. They had the secret of eternal life, and they knew very well who the giver of that life was. Their mission was to tell everyone about this true God, this king who would bring His kingdom to the earth, a kingdom without equal, of joy and peace never seen before. They were willing to give up everything, to suffer, to be mocked, to be imprisoned, and even to die.

They were the first heroes of the faith, the ones on whom the columns of the church were built. Thousands of years ago they fulfilled their purpose, and today they are captured in the pages of this book.

Stephen vs. Saul (20 minutes)

Give your students a blank piece of paper and the following instructions. They must read the verses that follow and draw the two characters being described based on the reading. Be sure to remind them not to draw anything inappropriate. You can download and print the following picture from the link we give you below.

Download the daily "Family" readings from www. e625.com/lessons.

Stephen and Paul couldn't be more opposite. Stephen was full of faith, of the Holy

Spirit, and of the grace and power of God (6:8). He's even described as having the face of an angel (6:15).

Saul, or Paul, witnessed how Christians were being killed and was in agreement (8:1). He pursued Christians and arrested them (8:3). He issued death threats against the disciples (9:1).

But God had other plans. Plans that we cannot humanly understand.

Acts 9:3-31.
Stephen had to die at Saul's feet, and Stephen fulfilled his part. Saul, whom we later come to know as Paul, had a wrong idea about who God was. He was Jewish and he knew the law of Moses very well, but he believed that Christians were against it, as he had not experienced the living God. When God presented Himself to Saul and made Himself known, Saul turned completely. But he did not stop being who he was. With the same passion and desire he'd expressed before, he now became a disciple of Jesus. Christ Himself said of Saul: "I have chosen him to proclaim my name among the nations, before kings, and to the people of Israel." (Acts 9:15). God's plan is always better than ours. He uses our talents and our personalities to reach where others cannot, to manage what not everyone can, to achieve what only each one of us individually can achieve.

Thanks to the people who were willing to die to spread the good news of salvation through Jesus, to preach His resurrection for eternal life, the church began to spread throughout the Middle East. When Stephen died, many believers dispersed to nearby and not-so-nearby cities carrying the good news wherever they went. They worked miracles and taught with great wisdom, each according to the grace that the Holy Spirit gave him. They had to suffer torture and prison, but they also experienced the power of God delivering them from evil to fulfill His purpose. Every one of them was willing to die for the cause.

Closing (10 minutes)

Think and draw. On the back of the paper, instruct everyone to draw themselves secretly.

What are your strengths?
-You make friends quickly.
-You like to smile.
-You are good at a sport.
-You are an artist.
-You know how to listen.

-You give good advice.
-You know how to ask for forgiveness.
-You can tell when someone is not doing well.
-You have a good memory.
-Other. (Try to think about what you know or can perceive from your students.)

What things do you see in your character today that you wish God would give a better purpose?
-You get angry easily.
-You are quick to insult.
-You sometimes shut down and won't communicate.
-You have fears.
-You don't feel comfortable in your body.
-You are too quick to respond.
-You feel less worthy than others.
-You lie to or fool adults easily.
-You care too much about what others say about you.
-You need the affection of others to feel good.
-Other. (Try to think about what you know or can perceive from your students.)

God can do things you can't imagine with your strengths and weaknesses. He wants to use you and give purpose to your life. The Holy Spirit can change us completely. In God we have new life.

Close with a prayer that includes confession of faith, repentance, and surrender, requesting the power of the Holy Spirit.

Download the daily "Family" readings from www. e625.com/lessons.

Chapters 13-28: Taking the message to the ends of the world.

Welcome and introductory questions (10 minutes)

Before starting the lesson and after greeting your middle schoolers, take three minutes to ask three non-personal questions, designed to be inviting and unintimidating. These can be directed toward the whole class, or you can call on someone you know will be comfortable answering in front of the whole group:

1. What is the longest trip you've ever taken?
2. What's a trip you would like to take? How long would it last? How many stops would you make? Why those places?
3. Who would you take with you on those trips? Why?

After Saul met God, his goals changed completely. From persecuting, imprisoning, and killing Christians, he went on to become one of the disciples who influenced society the most, proclaiming the message of salvation. Just as God had used Ananias in chapter 9:15-16, God used Paul to speak to common people and to kings. Paul knew the law of Moses well, and he now also had the Holy Spirit to give him life.

Saul never stopped having a passion for the Lord and a desire to please Him. Now he had a purpose from God, and he put all his knowledge, strength, and faith in Him. That is why Paul embarked on a lifelong journey.

Postcards from Paul (20-30 minutes)

Prepare several sets of 18 cardboard cards, as if they were postcards, one set for each team that plays. On each of the 18 cards write "Greetings from…" and the name of one of the cities. Each set must have all 18 cities for each team. Write in the following cities, one on each "postcard":

Greetings from....
Cyprus.
Antioch.
Iconium.
Lystra.
Derbe.

Jerusalem.
Macedonia.
Philippi.
Thessalonica.
Berea.
Athens.
Corinth.
Ephesus.
Greece.
Troas.
Caesarea.
Malta.
Rome.

You can divide your students into group as follows:
To divide your students into two or more groups of approximately 10 students each, look for as many photos of world-famous monuments or structures as there are groups you need to form. They can be photos of the Eiffel Tower, the Brooklyn Bridge, the Sydney Opera House, or some that you like from your own city. If you need to divide students into two groups, just choose two pictures; if you need four groups, then you will need four pictures. Download the pictures and print ten or more copies of each one. When you are ready to play, make sure you have the same number of copies of each photo and that there is only one for each student. Put all these pictures in a bag and have each student take one without looking. Then they will join a group with those who have the same image.

If the groups are uneven, don't worry! Just make sure that everyone is on a team. Once the groups are separated, give each team one of the sets of 18 cards that you prepared with the names of the cities, and one or more Bibles. At the signal, they must put the cards in order, listing them in the order of Paul's travels. The team that finishes first wins the first hundred points. For the other team to have a chance of revenge, the game now becomes a little more complicated. Now give students the following list of names to find in the stories of Paul's travels. Whoever manages to correctly place the names on the postcards with the biblical quote where those names are found will receive 200 points. If possible, try to have a prize prepared that can be shared among the team players.

Agrippa and Bernice.
Ananias.
Apollos.
Aquila and Priscilla.
Bar-Jesus.

Demetrius.
Dionysus and Damaris.
Erastus.
Philip.
Jason.
John Mark.
Judas.
Julius.
Lydia.
Publius.
Silas.
Tertullus.
Timothy.

Reflection (10 minutes)

Saul, also called Paul, had been a persecutor of Christians. With a great zeal for the law that he knew, he tried to exterminate the "new religion." But God, who knows all things and knows very well who we are, had other plans for Paul. In the hands of the Lord, Paul was an essential tool for the early church, and thanks to his tenacity, passion, and knowledge he managed to plant dozens of churches. He made thousands of faithful disciples of the Lord who took the gospel to the entire world. It wasn't easy. He suffered torture, prison, mockery, was shipwrecked, and was even bitten by a snake! But Paul knew very well who he was, who he worked for, and where he was going.

The Lord calls all of us, in whichever condition we find ourselves, regardless of whether we feel adequate or not. He promises to be with us, to equip us with His Holy Spirit, and to have our back in every situation. Does He promise us that everything will be a bed or roses? No! He tells us instead that, just as Jesus suffered to free us from evil, we will also suffer for others. But His reward is much greater than anything that the world can give us.

> **Questions to reflect on:**
> Ask each of these questions, and tell your students to think about the answers silently.
> What does it mean for God to call someone?
> Is the Lord calling you? What do you think is His calling for you?
> Do you think He can use you just as you are?
> Are you willing to follow Him wherever He leads you? Where do you think that place is?
> What will be your answer to Him?

Closing (5-10 minutes)

Paul and his disciples were the first missionaries of the gospel of God's kingdom, but many others have taken the message of salvation to the entire world. Thousands of people have suffered and died in unknown lands, far from their families, for the sake of the gospel. Just like Jesus, they gave their lives to bring the Lord's salvation message to those who otherwise would have never known Him.

The Lord may call us to go to faraway places, or to speak to those around us. He may call us to share with words, with art, with videos, or with any talent He has given us. What's important is to say yes and to obey Him. Our faith may be what leads us to a wonderfully supernatural life at the hand of the God of miracles.

Close this lesson by praying for those who will be called to go to neighboring nations, and for those who will carry the message of salvation to their own hometowns. Ask for the power of the Holy Spirit to fill their hearts, strengthen their faith, and bring them conviction, as He did with Paul. You can search for the video or song "If I don't do it myself" by Marcos Witt, or another song better known to your students. You can also find and show a video with images illustrating the need to bring the Word of God to those who have not heard it.

Download the daily "Family" readings from www. e625.com/lessons.

Lesson 31 > JAMES

This book begins as a letter and ends as a sermon. The author is believed to be Jesus' half-brother (Mark 6:3). James was known as "James the Just" because of his devotion to justice. His letter to the scattered Christians after Stephen's death emphasizes putting what they learned into practice. It is a rich letter full of content that is essential for a life with God. James wrote with the authority of one who had personally seen the resurrected Christ. With his devotion to direct and deep statements, James brings us a practical message that emphasizes godly conduct.

Welcome and introductory questions (10 minutes)

Before starting the lesson and after greeting your middle schoolers, take three minutes to ask three non-personal questions, designed to be inviting and unintimidating. These can be directed toward the whole class, or you can call on someone you know will be comfortable answering in front of the whole group:

1. What is faith? How is faith born?
2. What is a trial? What things are tested in a trial? What were the most difficult trials you have experienced?
3. How does faith help us in trials?

Chair stilt race! (20 minutes)

As we all know, middle schoolers love risks and adventure, so let's go! Assemble two teams as follows: ask two students to come forward and cover their eyes with a blindfold. Ask the rest of the students to form a circle around them without talking. These two players, blindfolded, must choose their teammates. They cannot ask questions or choose two people sitting next to each other. They have to cross from one side of the circle to the other looking for teammates. When touched by one of the blindfolded players, students must join that person's side. The circle should shrink as the players are chosen.

Once the teams are formed, one player from each team will come forward to perform the skill. That representative will have to walk some distance (if you have time, add some obstacles) with two chairs tied to him, one on each leg, with the student standing on the chair's seat. The easiest way to do it is with thick tape. They'll also carry an inflated balloon in their mouth! Yes! It's a race, with chairs as stilts! Use chairs that do not fold. Two teammates will stand at each player's sides, but they cannot touch the player unless there is a safety risk. Whoever arrives first wins. If you don't have many students, they can all compete.

If you have too many, create several teams, or you can have relays. You can change the difficulty level according to your students' skills, making the course longer or more difficult as needed. You can also change the chairs for other objects, but make them unexpected and even ridiculous.

Questions at the end of the race:
1. To those who were not on the chairs:
- What do you think was the most difficult?

2. To those who had the chairs tied to their legs:
- What was the first thing you thought when we explained the game?
- What part was the most difficult? Why?

Introduction
In our daily life we place faith in hundreds of things. That may seem strange, but we live by constantly exercising faith. For example: a chair. We sit with faith, confident that the chair will support us and we will not fall. We saw this in the race we ran with the chairs. We knew the chairs would support us. We didn't know if we could walk with them, but we knew the chairs could support our weight. That's faith in action. Another very common example is a light switch: when we flip the switch, we have faith that there will be light. Again, we exercise faith with actions. We would be surprised or worried if the chair breaks or the light doesn't turn on, because we'd know that meant something was wrong. Today we will learn how practicing our faith in Jesus helps us learn to trust Him and alleviates our doubts.

Book review (10 minutes)
Separate the large group into five smaller groups. Give each group a Bible and assign each one a chapter from James.

Download from www.e625.com/lessons the complimentary materials for this section

When class started we talked about what faith and trials were like for each of us. No one is safe from trials or difficulties. Jesus suffered the worst ones! Jesus Himself said, "A time is coming and in fact has come when you will be scattered, each to your own home. You will leave me all alone. Yet I am not alone, for my Father is with me. I have told you these things, so that in me you may have peace. In this world you will have trouble. But take heart! I have overcome the world" (John 16:32-33).

Jesus is referring to the time when He would be handed over to die on the cross. When He was facing His worst trials, even His friends abandoned Him, but He could be confident that God was with Him and that He would not be alone. We can learn to trust God with complete security, just like when we turn on the light and know it will turn on, or when we sit and we know the chair will support us. Although we cannot avoid difficulties, we can endure them with courage because we know Jesus has overcome anything that this world can throw at us, and God is always with us.

Conclusion (15 minutes)

For the explanation and conclusion of James' book you must download, print, or build the dynamic table that you will find in the complimentary materials for this lesson. In addition to the table, you will find the explanation of each part and their respective colors. It is important that you prepare it in advance and study the instructions because, as students work, you can explain the concept of faith, works, trials, and consequences.

Is faith useful if we don't act on it?
No, our actions must show our faith.

Are good actions enough without faith in Jesus?
No, only Jesus can save us, if we believe in Him, through our faith in His salvation.

Faith needs knowledge of God to produce not only more faith but also action. As we act we will be tested. By going through hard times and trials firm in the knowledge of God, we develop a resoluteness with which the Lord promises to help us become mature and complete. With God, we lack nothing! What more can we ask for? Just praise the Lord who not only strengthens us for hard times, but rewards us with much more than the world can give us!

Additional closing songs

Consider closing with a worship song that your group likes and emphasizes themes from today's lesson.

Download the daily "Family" readings from www. e625.com/lessons.

The letter of Galatians was written by Paul to the churches in the area or region of Galatia, which had both Jewish and non-Jewish (Gentile) residents. At first they had understood the grace of God and the origin of salvation, but now many of their teachers wanted to impose Jewish law on non-Jews as a requirement to becoming Christians. More specifically, they wanted to impose circumcision on men. As the Galatians were starting to believe that they needed to follow these Jewish laws, Paul wrote to them to defend justification by faith. The central theme of the book is freedom in Christ versus the legalism of the tradition and law.

Welcome and introductory questions (10 minutes)

Before starting the lesson and after greeting your middle schoolers, take three minutes to ask three non-personal questions, designed to be inviting and unintimidating.

These can be directed toward the whole class, or you can call on someone you know will be comfortable answering in front of the whole group:

1. What laws do you think help us to have order but at the same time limit us?
2. Are there laws that give people freedoms you don't agree with?
3. (Be careful with the responses you give as examples as you may introduce sensitive topics.)
4. What wars or battles were fought to abolish certain laws?

There are laws that bring order to society, and others that have caused wars. In the letter to the Galatians, Paul opposed the slavery caused by the imposition of many laws that had nothing to do with being free in Christ. This led to a great revolution.

Let's see if you can! (15 minutes)

Three participants will come to the front. The objective is for these three participants to write the verse of Galatians 5:1 on the blackboard, on a poster, or on a piece of paper. Another student or teacher will dictate the verse from the other end of the room (or far enough away to have to raise their voice). As the participants begin to write the verse, the rest of the students will start making up rules on how they should do it. For example: jumping on one foot, with one hand behind their back, with one eye closed, with their left hand, etc. The rules will add up. The student who first manages to finish writing the complete verse is the winner.

Worksheet "Freedom vs. Slavery" (30 minutes)

Give each student a copy of the worksheet for everyone to complete. They will each also need a pencil and a Bible. You can have groups of two or three students work together.

Download from www.e625.com/lessons the complimentary materials for this section

Answers for the teacher: Freedom vs. Slavery.

1- Allow time for several students to give their opinion. No one thinks of slavery as something pleasant. Slavery means that someone dominates us and we can't do anything about it. The slave has a master. In this case the masters are sin and the consequences of sin. In the book of Galatians, the Jews were used to obeying many laws in order to please God. Those laws dictated what they should eat, their behavior, their rituals, everything! It was impossible to obey every law perfectly. That is why we needed Christ: so that in Him all the law would be fulfilled and He would free us and justify us before God. To justify means to make righteous. Galatians 3:21-24 says, *"Is the law, therefore, opposed to the promises of God? Absolutely not! For if a law had been given that could impart life, then righteousness would certainly have come by the law. But Scripture has locked up everything under the control of sin, so that what was promised, being given through faith in Jesus Christ, might be given to those who believe. Before the coming of this faith, we were held in custody under the law, locked up until the faith that was to come would be revealed. So the law was our guardian until Christ came that we might be justified by faith."*

2- Allow time for several students to give their opinion. To be free is to have nothing that binds or enslaves us, and that is what Christ accomplished on the cross. He made us righteous and perfect before God. What for? To enable us to approach Him in a parent-child relationship. God always wanted to be close to us, but our evil deeds kept us away from Him. Jesus, who had NO sin, became unjust and paid our debt by justifying Himself before God, allowing each of us to have a personal relationship with Him. Galatians 3:26 says, *"So in Christ Jesus you are all children of God through faith,"* and Galatians 4:7 says, *"So you are no longer a slave, but God's child; and since you are his child, God has made you also an heir."*

3- Allow time for several students to give their opinion. In the case of the Galatians, the law that was imposed on the Jews made them slaves, because they said that the way to earn salvation was through compliance with many rules. Galatians 3:10 says, *"For all who rely on the works of the law are under a curse, as it is written: "Cursed is everyone who does not continue to do everything written in the Book of the Law."*

According to the law "the things we have to do" are the rules that enslave us. But Christ came to give us freedom. We can have joy knowing that we do not have to do or pay anything to obtain salvation.

4- A. After some time, allow students to respond: What are things that make us slaves? What stops us from enjoying freedom in Jesus? We enslave ourselves with lies: We are not attractive enough, intelligent enough, talented enough. We let others enslave us when we listen to them saying we are good for nothing. We allow lies to make us forget who we are to God and how much we are worth to Him. Some of us think we have to behave in a certain way in order to please God, our parents, and Church leaders, while the truth is that Jesus wants us to accept His goodness and to understand that no lie can enslave us.

4- B. To not submit again is to not put back on the chains that tie us to the rules of humans, the lies of Satan, and the laws of religion. God has already forgiven us through Jesus' sacrifice. We are the most important thing to Him, and He gave us the freedom of not having to do anything to be saved or to be loved by the Father. Why would we want to put back on the chains that bind us? Why fall back into the sin that enslaves us?

5- After they answer A and B, read Galatians 5:16-18: "*So I say, walk by the Spirit, and you will not gratify the desires of the flesh. For the flesh desires what is contrary to the Spirit, and the Spirit what is contrary to the flesh….But if you are led by the Spirit, you are not under the law.*" The law and the rules show us that we are sinning, according to verse 19: depraved sexual acts, idolatry, witchcraft, hatred, fighting, jealousy, anger, rivalry, etc. But what happens when we allow ourselves to be guided by the Spirit of God is quite the opposite. So why let ourselves be enslaved by the things the world tells us "are normal, fashionable, in style"? They produce death and slavery, but the guidance of the Spirit of God brings life. Galatians 5:25 says: "*Since we live by the Spirit, let us keep in step with the Spirit.*"

Closing, and time for personal reflection (5 minutes)

Think about anything that is enslaving you or preventing you from enjoying freedom in Christ. Go back to point 5A and examine yourself. Write anything that is enslaving you on the back of the worksheet and ask God to deliver you from it. The world disguises itself as good and makes us fall as slaves to it. Religion enslaves us by making us think we are doing what's right. But the true love of God gives us freedom. By living our lives pleasing God through the guidance of the Holy Spirit, we can freely enjoy every minute.

Download the daily "Family" readings from www.e625.com/lessons.

The author of the two letters to the church in Thessalonica was Paul. With Paul were his assistants and traveling companions, Silas and Timothy. It is believed that Paul wrote these letters while they were in Corinth between 51 and 52 AD. In the first letter to the Thessalonians Paul addresses the topic of hope in Christ and His second coming. In his second letter, he describes the effects of Christ's second coming, the glorification of believers, and God's judgment of unbelievers.

Welcome and introductory questions (10 minutes)

Before starting the lesson and after greeting your middle schoolers, take three minutes to ask three non-personal questions, designed to be inviting and unintimidating. These can be directed toward the whole class, or you can call on someone you know will be comfortable answering in front of the whole group:

1. What types of messages do parents write to their children when they are away from them for a while, maybe for a few days?
2. Do your parents send you messages while you are apart from each other? Only for a longer trip or throughout the average day?
3. Is there a question your parents ask you every day? What is it?

If your parents are like mine, their messages usually consist of things like: "Grab a coat, it's cold," "Don't forget to do your homework," "Call me when you get there," "Are you having a good time?" "Do you want me to pick you up?" and "I love you." Some parents may write these and other messages, to know how you are doing, if you need help, etc. They do it with true concern and affection. Many years ago the way to obtain information about loved ones who were far away was through letters.

"The Messenger Timothy" (25 minutes)

Divide your team into groups as follows:
Prepare a piece of cardboard in different colors. As students arrive, have an assistant write the names of each student on a color, alternating evenly between the colors to make sure the teams have equal numbers of players. Then, when you get to this part of the meeting, divide students according to the colors, calling out the names that appear in each one.

On one side of the room, place all the teams and give them the images that correspond with this lesson.

On the other side of the room, set up a table and a printout of each of the messages that follow, each one written on a separate piece of paper. The players will run to the table, grab a message, read it aloud, and together decide to which image they belong. The team that completes the challenge first is the winner.

Message 1: 1 Thessalonians 4:3-6
Message 2: 1 Thessalonians 4:7-8
Message 3: 1 Thessalonians 4:9-10
Message 4: 1 Thessalonians 4:11-12
Message 5: 1 Thessalonians 5:14-15
Message 6: 1 Thessalonians 5:16-18
Message 7: 2 Thessalonians 2:15-16
Message 8: 2 Thessalonians 3:7-10
Message 9: 2 Thessalonians 3:13

Download from www.e625.com/lessons the complimentary materials for this section

Reflection

Both letters to the Thessalonians feature the apostle Paul's spiritual children. They were a group of people in the city of Thessalonica who had converted to Christ and believed wholeheartedly. The reason Paul and his assistant Silas were concerned about them and wrote them two letters is that at that time, Christians were persecuted to death for preaching that Jesus was the only king. Under this threat of persecution, some were tempted to give up Jesus' teachings and live a life of disobedience, while others were getting confused by wrong teachings from false teachers. The apostle Paul writes to them to make sure that they are following the teachings of Jesus, and that they are living a life that reflects those teachings. They loved these people so much that they sent Timothy, a young assistant, to visit them to bring them news of them. Timothy became known as "the messenger."

Paul, like a good spiritual father, took the opportunity to write to them. He was proud of them and he wanted to affirm what they had learned and encourage them to continue following the teachings of Jesus "more and more" each day. He challenged them this way because the Christian life has to be one of continuous growth, as each day we get to know Jesus better and better understand how to live in Him.

Application

The images help us see how these recommendations from Paul are significant for us today.

Give each student a copy of "Paul's Messages for Me" to complete when they finish the previous activity, and then review each image with them. In the second column, have students write their challenges, and in the third column they can write how they can comply with Paul's advice.

Download from www.e625.com/lessons the complimentary materials for this section

To lead a life that pleases God, we need to ask ourselves: What would Jesus do? He is our greatest example. To live a Christian life is to live within God's will. When God wants something for us, it is always for our own good. To obey him is to honor His will and His purpose for us.

Paul helps his disciples focus on what is important and what is good. All our actions must reflect who we are. Many things were distracting the believers in Thessalonica, so Paul encouraged them to refocus.

Download the daily "Family" readings from www.e625.com/lessons.

As the first verse says, the author of this letter is Paul. He probably wrote it in 55 AD from the city of Ephesus, during his third missionary journey.

Paul was hoping to visit the Corinthians soon. The letter to the church in Corinth focuses on helping believers to be mature in Christ, correcting some false teachings that were entering the church and reminding them of the sacrifice on the cross, especially the resurrection of Jesus for the sanctification of believers in Christ.

Welcome and introductory questions (10 minutes)

Before starting the lesson and after greeting your middle schoolers, take three minutes to ask three non-personal questions, designed to be inviting and unintimidating. These can be directed toward the whole class, or you can call on someone you know will be comfortable answering in front of the whole group:

1. What is a church?
2. What kind of people make up a church?
3. Is the church perfect? Why not? What would a perfect church look like?

In Corinth there were several leaders that perhaps today we would call pastors or elders. The people in the church had a tendency to compare and contrast them. Does this sound familiar to you? This type of comparison is a tendency that arises from immature human thinking. Paul found out what was happening and wanted to help this community of Christians live lives focused on Christ. To do this, Paul sent Timothy (1 Cor. 4:17) to remind the Corinthians about how they should behave, and what Paul's teachings were regarding these matters. In his first letter to the Corinthians, he reminded and taught the church at Corinth many things. We're going to focus on what is perhaps the most important thing he taught, because it helps us understand the essence of what the church is and should be.

Many members, one body (15-20 minutes)

For the next activity you will need modeling clay or play dough. If it's colorful, even better. Give each student a piece of clay, enough to create a human figure. Tell students they have 30 seconds to create what you instruct them to before they'll have to pass their creation on. They can't have any extra time, so they'll have to spend it wisely. Give them the signal to pass what they've made when their time is up, perhaps reminding them when 15 seconds are up. (This is a good exercise in time awareness.)

Give them the following instructions:

- Create ONLY the head shape (not eyes, ears, lips, etc.) and the hair of your doll.
- Then pass your doll to the student to your right.
- To the head they gave you, add the doll's torso.
- Pass it to the right.
- Add legs to the torso and head.
- Pass it to the right.
- Now add the arms.
- Pass it to the right.

And so on with the details of the entire body, face, ears, clothing, accessories, etc. You can make the doll as simple or as complicated as you want.

The last student must give the character a name and a special power: To be able to fly, jump high, run at the speed of light, laser beam eyes, super strength, invisibility, etc. Don't let students repeat the same superpowers. Have students write the name and special power on a piece of paper to put up next to where their dolls will be displayed.

Ask:
Why that particular superpower?
If you had the same superpower as the doll you made, what would you do with it?
Variation: If you do not have access to modeling clay, give a sheet of white paper to each student and something to draw with. Then give the same instructions with them drawing the doll instead of molding it.

Reflection (15 minutes)
Don't spend too much time on each question: Give students time to reflect, but move on quickly so that the meaning is understood and you don't lose their attention.

Read one verse each from 1 Corinthians 12:12-31.

How is Paul explaining to the Corinthians what the church is?
How are we that "body"?
Is each and every one necessary? Why?
What are the gifts and services provided within the church?
What are the gifts and services provided outside of the church?
Who is the best member? Why?
Why are different "body parts" needed?

Which part are you? (unanswered)

To be the body of Christ, we need everyone. Why? Because not all of us can do the same things, nor do we all have the same talents, abilities, or gifts from God. The church is similar to the dolls we made. It will not be perfect because we are not perfect, but in God we can become one, with Christ as the head to give us direction. Many times we mistake the services provided inside the church as the only ones that are necessary and useful, but in reality they are a small part. Jesus spent time in the synagogues teaching and learning, but almost all His ministry was on the streets, going from place to place preaching the kingdom of God, caring for the sick, comforting those who had lost loved ones, freeing the oppressed, feeding the poor, and even playing with the children.

We need leaders, pastors, and teachers, but we also need other members of the body to live in harmony. If each one was in our own place, fulfilling our role according to our talents, we could live as Paul says in 1 Corinthians 1:10: In harmony, unity of spirit and thought. But for this to happen, Paul has an even better lesson: Starting with chapter 12:31b: "And yet I will show you the most excellent way." Read 1 Corinthians 13:1-3.

Why are these gifts useless without love? We may have the most spectacular superpower in the world, but if we do not love our neighbor as Jesus loved us, it is of no use. Our superpowers are worth nothing unless they serve others.

True love (5 minutes)

Download from www.e625.com/lessons and print a copy of this sheet for each student.

Circle the words you think describe true love.

Then read 1 Corinthians 13:4-10.

Which of the words that you circled are found in Paul's teaching?
Which others are missing from the text?
Can this perfect love be real? What does it mean to achieve perfect love?

Closing (5 minutes)

Paul teaches us in 1 Corinthians that each and every one of us is special and important. The Lord has given us abilities, passions, talents, and gifts to use to bring others to Him and to serve and bless the people around us, both inside and outside the church.

Sometimes we forget this. That's when we begin to see our task with human eyes, which leads to confusion, division, and pride. Instead of being a blessing, we hurt those we should love. We must love our brothers and sisters and those who are not yet our brothers and sisters. Many things will happen and many changes will transpire, but true love remains. It is not easy to love in the way Paul describes, but we know if we do, everything will be different.

Selfishness leads us to focus on ourselves, but love focuses on others. When love is reciprocal, we coexist perfectly.

Close in prayer, thanking God that we are able to be part of His body. Pray for your students to discover their call, talents, and gifts from God so they can fulfill their purpose within the body.

Above all else, pray that they can love and be loved with the perfect love that only God can give through His Holy Spirit.

Download the daily "Family" readings from www. e625.com/lessons.

Paul writes this second letter to the Corinthians approximately a year after his first letter to the believers in this city. False prophets had interfered within the church of Corinth and incited them to turn against Paul, so the apostle immediately went to visit them. His visit was a disaster, as one of the brothers insulted him. Saddened by the lack of loyalty, Paul returned to Ephesus. From there wrote harshly to the Corinthians. This is an intensely personal letter, a battle against those who attacked his authority. Even so, Paul continues teaching with his heart in his hand.

Welcome and introductory questions (10 minutes)

Before starting the lesson and after greeting your middle schoolers, take three minutes to ask three non-personal questions, designed to be inviting and unintimidating. These can be directed toward the whole class, or you can call on someone you know will be comfortable answering in front of the whole group:

1. Of the inspiring messages you've seen on social media, which one do you like most? Why?
2. Have you ever created one of your own? What is it?
3. How have the situations you experience on a daily basis helped you to think of phrases that can encourage others?

Note: In advance, in case your group doesn't have answers, search social media for inspirational phrases.

Paul has left the city of Corinth sad because of some confrontations. His first letter had been somewhat harsh, and on his return to Rome he decided not to stop in Corinth again. He was still somewhat hurt and did not want to act on impulse. He then writes them a letter full of feelings and love. We could make many memes and inspiring phrases from this letter.

Paul's posts (30 minutes)

Prepare in advance as many art materials as you can, such as colored paper, patterned paper, old magazines, markers, different types of stickers, scissors, glue, etc. Don't forget to ask your students' parents for help.

On a table, place the verses from the list below, printed on strips of paper. Then ask your students to choose one and make a poster depicting Paul's teaching as given in the verse, using the art supplies provided. Then display them on the wall of your meeting room or church. Have everyone read them and vote on which one they like the most.

They don't necessarily have to copy the verse; they can change the words to make them rhyme or to paraphrase what is said. They can choose part of or the whole verse, but they must not change the meaning.

Have fun!

2 Corinthians 1:4
2 Corinthians 1:20
2 Corinthians 1:22
2 Corinthians 3:5-6
2 Corinthians 3:17-18
2 Corinthians 4:5-6
2 Corinthians 4:16
2 Corinthians 5:5
2 Corinthians 5:14-16
2 Corinthians 5:17
2 Corinthians 5:21
2 Corinthians 6:2
2 Corinthians 6:6
2 Corinthians 6:8-10
2 Corinthians 7:10
2 Corinthians 9:6-9
2 Corinthians 10:17-18
2 Corinthians 12:9-10
2 Corinthians 13:4
2 Corinthians 13:11

Variation: you can split students into teams and divide all the verses among them so that they can make them in their pictures. You can also let them make their art on digital devices and then post them on a social network. We recommend that you do this in a way that highlights the effort and creativity. After they read and review all the artwork, ask students to vote for the following:

Luego que lean y revisen todos los carteles, pídeles que voten:
- Best message. Why?
- Best decoration.
- The one they would like their friends to see the most. Why?
- The one they would like their parents to see the most. Why?
- The one that would motivate someone who's sad.
- The one that would work best for someone who has behaved with pride.
- The one that's most useful to me today.

Paul wrote to the Corinthian church after they'd had some difficult exchanges, but he told them in a loving way how he felt, and how knowledge in the Lord would unite them and restore them. He reminded them about the things that are important, and the ones that are not.

Read 2 Corinthians 2:1-11.

On his previous visit, Paul had experienced issues with some of the members of that church. Paul was uneasy. He knew that, although it was necessary to rebuke those who had caused problems, it was also important to restore them and continue loving them. This would show them the love of God and bring out the love of God living in them so they could learn to walk in the truth.

- Have you had a problem with someone you thought was your friend?
- How did you solve it?
- Are you still angry with a friend?
- How does Paul say we should solve situations like this?
- How can Satan take advantage of a bad situation and of failure to restore relationships?

The motivations behind our messages are important. Being in good relationships, even with those who have hurt us in the past, is also important, because otherwise anger and resentment grow within us. When we recognize God's power it feeds our soul and encourages those around us.

Close with a prayer thanking God for all His love and goodness. Pray for your students to discover new ways to bless their friends with messages of love and encouragement in the Word of God. Pray that they can also restore their relationships, and not give way to the devil.

Download the daily "Family" readings from www.e625.com/lessons.

The name of this epistle refers to its recipients, the believers at the church located in the capital of the Roman Empire. Paul is the author of this epistle. He was a Roman citizen from the city of Tarsus. Paul was responsible for the spread of the gospel throughout the Empire. After returning from Jerusalem to Rome, he was falsely accused, beaten, and taken into Roman custody. After a short period of freedom in which he was able to travel, he was once again arrested, and died a martyr in Rome around 66-67 AD. Paul wrote to the church at Rome from Corinth around 56 AD. This letter is above all a doctrinal letter, and it declares that the only thing that justifies the human sinner before God is faith in the work of Jesus on the cross, which sanctifies us and reconciles us with the eternal Father. In chapters 1 to 11, the theological truths of the doctrine of justification are presented, while in chapters 12 to 16 Paul writes about practical matters in the life of the church.

Welcome and introductory questions (10 minutes)

Before starting the lesson and after greeting your middle schoolers, take three minutes to ask three non-personal questions, designed to be inviting and unintimidating. These can be directed toward the whole class, or you can call on someone you know will be comfortable answering in front of the whole group:

1. Have you ever been caught misbehaving? What did you do, and how did you get caught?
2. Have you ever justified something you did by saying it was "because everyone else was doing it"?
3. Have you ever been punished while others got away with it, even though you had all done something wrong? How did it happen?

We've all been caught in less-than-honorable moments, and sometimes we've suffered the consequences. It's likely that at some point you have taken the blame for something that someone else did—maybe you were the only one who got caught while everyone else ran away. Or maybe you've been the one who got away while someone else took the blame.

Have you ever been in a situation where someone tried to take the blame for something that wasn't their fault?

Who would do that? At the end of the day, if someone did something bad, that person should be the one to pay the consequences, right? That's what adults always tell us, isn't it?

Paul shares about the opposite of this in his letter to Rome, reminding the Christians there of a story of sacrifice, undeserved punishment, and love.

Tell me a story (15-20 minutes)

Ask your students to stand in a circle. If possible mix them up so that it is girl, boy, girl, boy, etc. Give each student a piece of paper and a pencil and ask them to write the following list:

- A place (Paris, the bathroom, the park, the school, etc.).
- An object (a cup, a door, a mirror, a tablecloth, etc.).
- A mode of transportation (a car, a plane, a train, skates, etc.).
- A part of the body (mouth, leg, ankle, fingers, etc.).
- An article of clothing (socks, shirt, hat, gloves, etc.).
- An action (run, jump, fly, eat, sleep, etc.).

Once everyone has their list we will create a story together. The first student begins by telling us the beginning of the story: "Once upon a time," "The legend tells us," "It was a gray day," etc., using the first word they wrote (the place).

For example the first player may say, "Once upon a time there was a boy named John who was in Paris and…", leaving the sentence unfinished. The second player will continue the story using their second word: "and he drank a cup of coffee that was getting cold in the kitchen." The third player continues the sequence using their third word, and so on until all the players have used their words or the story cannot continue. (It will probably never make sense.)

- What is your favorite story and why?
- Do stories always make sense? Why?
- What about true stories? Do they always make sense?

Many real-life stories have been captured in books because they are unusual and wonderful. Some are very sad, such as stories of captivity or natural disasters, of wars, slaves, or prisoners; others are magnificent achievements, but they always remain within the boundaries of human possibility.

The most wonderful story ever told (20 minutes)

Cut out four large circles or squares made out of construction paper, in the following colors: black, red, yellow, and pink. Then, as appropriate, write on the circles the titles and verses below. You or a helper will read the verses as if you are telling a story to small children, with plenty of gestures, voices, and emotion.

Paul reminds the Romans of the greatest story in human history, which consists of four chapters:

Chapter 1: Deserved death.
Color black: Romans 1:18-23, 29-32; 3:9-20; 2:16.
Sinful human nature: Sin separates us from God. Only Jesus Christ can reconcile us to the Father.

Chapter 2: For love nothing is impossible.
Color red: Romans 3:21-26; 5:1-2, 6-9.
Justification by faith: Sin makes us slaves and brings condemnation to all humans, but through faith in Jesus Christ we have freedom.

Chapter 3: A new surname.
Color yellow: Romans 5:18-19; 6:1-14.
Sanctification: Through the blood of Jesus Christ we are glorified and set apart for God as a holy nation.

Chapter 4: Back home.
Color pink: Romans 5:10-11; 8:1, 4-17, 29-35, 38-39.
Reconciliation: Jesus' sacrifice on the cross breaks the veil that prohibited us from entering the presence of God and thus restores our relationship with the Father.

Note: If you can, put together a small book of colors for each student with the verses written on each page so they can follow along and keep the book afterward. After each reading you can say in your own words what each verse means, but the verses pretty much speak for themselves. If while writing the verses you see the need for "connecting words," don't be afraid to add them, but make sure you keep the message..

Closing (10 minutes)

This story was written almost 2,000 years ago but it applies to all of us today. When Jesus wrote His script in blood, He was thinking about you and me. He saw our faces and knew our names. That's why He didn't get off the cross. He knew that His sacrifice was worth it for the lives of His friends and of all humans across history.

None of us can deny God's unconditional love, but neither can we remain the same when knowing Him. No one can reject Jesus' desire to take our place on the cross, but neither can we despise Him by turning our back on Him after He died in our place. God wanted so much to speak to us again, to share His wisdom again, to hear our prayers, that He did not hesitate to send the only One who could rescue us. Yet, in giving up His most precious treasure for us, He left it up to us to decide whether to accept His gift or refuse it.

What is your answer? Are you going to leave your role in this story unfulfilled?

Close with a prayer of repentance, surrender, and gratitude for the sacrifice of Jesus Christ on the cross. Be thankful for this wonderful story that changes our lives and the lives of all humans. Bless your students and ask the Holy Spirit to work within them.

Download the daily "Family" readings from www.e625.com/lessons.

Ephesians belongs to the group of letters that Paul wrote during the time of his captivity in Rome, along with the letters to the Philippians, Colossians, and Philemon. They are known as the "prison epistles," or stories from captivity. The letter to the church of Ephesus was written between 60-62 AD. Along with Colossians, Ephesus emphasizes that the church is the body of Christ and He is the head. Paul affirms the identity of the believer in Christ, and how they should behave in this new identity.

Welcome and introductory questions (10 minutes)

Before starting the lesson and after greeting your middle schoolers, take three minutes to ask three non-personal questions, designed to be inviting and unintimidating. These can be directed toward the whole class, or you can call on someone you know will be comfortable answering in front of the whole group:

1. What wishes or messages are appropriate to put on someone's birthday card?
2. Why do we extend good wishes to others? On which occasions?
3. To whom do we usually extend good wishes? Why don't we share good wishes with strangers?

In this letter to the believers in the church at Ephesus, Paul writes to remind them of essential teachings while also giving them new advice. It seems he is very happy with his friends from this city. He offers them many good wishes, encouraging them to act in unity and to be strengthened in the truth of God.

Best wishes (15 minutes)

Prepare some blank papers in the shape and size of greeting cards, one for each student. Bring some colored markers and, if you can, stickers or old magazines from which students can cut out images. If you bring magazines, you will also need scissors and glue. Remember to ask parents or grandparents from the church for help providing needed supplies.

Print the following verses for students to read: Ephesians 1:16-20 and 3:16-19. Give students the supplies. Ask them to choose a message of good wishes and make a card based on it.

Paul most likely wanted to highlight the good work that the Ephesians were doing, and, as a good leader, he wanted to motivate them to be even better.

To start the letter to the Ephesians, Paul reminded them of the same message he taught the Romans. This message is foundational to understanding the kingdom of God. (Take out the book of colors that we made for the previous class.)

1. That we deserved death for our sins and selfishness.
2. That Jesus died to cleanse us and thus justify us in spite of our evil.
3. That through His blood He sanctified us, enabling us to be accepted again by God.
4. His work on the cross restored our relationship with God, who promised to never again separate us from His love.

Immediately after sharing this message, and after praising his friends at Ephesus and offering them good wishes, Paul reminds them why they have been such a good example.

Unity is strength (15 minutes)

You will need two large buckets of water, two empty buckets, and at least five plastic cups. Ask your students to divide into boys and girls.

Place the buckets of water at one end of the room. (This game will get the floor wet, so we recommend that you play on grass or on another surface that won't become slippery when wet to avoid accidents.) Place the empty buckets at the other end of the room. At the signal, both teams must transfer all the water from the full bucket to the empty bucket. The rule is that each student cannot touch more than one cup of water at a time.

The difference is that the boys must run one by one from one end to the other with only one cup of water at a time.

The girls will line up from one end to the other and pass each other the cups one by one. They just have to remember that they cannot have more than one cup in their hands at a time.

The girls' cups can come and go in the same line. If everything goes well, the idea is that the girls, if they manage to coordinate their efforts, will be able to transport the water faster, or the boys will realize that together they can carry the entire bucket while the other players hold the cups in their hands so as not to break the rule. If they don't discover this trick, after allowing a little excitement from the competition, you can whisper it in a player's ear.

Note: There are many other games that require teamwork you could also use. The idea is to highlight the importance of working together as one unit.

- What benefits does working as a team bring?
- What benefits do we obtain by working alone?
- What is the difference between working as a unit, knowing our place and what our role is, and working alone, trying to do everything ourselves?
- Do these two different ways of working exist within the church?
- How do they make us feel?
- How do you think God feels about these ways of existing in the world? Why?

Read Ephesians 2:11-16, 21-22; 4:2-6, 12-16.
What is God's plan for us as a church?
Paul talks about Jews and non-Jews. What different groups or categories of people do we have in the church today?
How is it that we can have so many differences, yet all be equal before God?
Can we tell someone we don't need them? Why?

Read Ephesians 5:1-2.

Sharing best wishes (5 minutes)

Now that we know we are to love each other as Christ loved us, take the card you made. Add to it a personal wish for someone in the group, something that you would never have thought of telling them before. Be honest, and don't make it a joke. Then look for that someone and give them the card.

Note: Have a few cards ready to give to students who don't receive one from their peers. You can also have an assistant at the door asking the students' parents and family members to write individual students a note of encouragement. This will require more work, but it can be done. Don't forget to ask for help from older people like grandparents, as they often want to invest in the younger generations at church.

Paul knows that it is not easy to behave as a body, in unity, because we are all different. That's why he doesn't just leave them the Ephesians with the burden, but also gives them the key to achieve it (Eph. 6:10-18).

Armor of God

Although this is something students might have done in a younger-age class, we have a good variation on the typical soldier wearing the armor of God.

Materials: Draw a large soldier (it does not need to be perfect). Then separately draw the parts of the armor to later dress the soldier. You will need a helmet, a shield, a breastplate, and a sword.

- On the shield, write: Faith.
- On the breastplate, write: Truth and Justice.
- On the helmet, write: Salvation.
- On the sword, write: Word of God.

Ask four volunteers, two boys and two girls, to come forward. Place your soldier on the wall. Give each student an item of the armor. Cover the eyes of the participants, one at a time, and they will try to dress the soldier, guided by the instructions of the rest of the group. Girls must guide girls and boys must guide boys. You can vote for who did the best job in dressing the soldier.

Closing (5 minutes)

Being part of the body of Christ is a privilege. He is our example and role model, and the people around us are also His children. There is no distinction or favoritism. Working as a team, motivating each other to be better, highlighting our strengths and encouraging those who feel weak will make us a healthy, strong body ready to win the battle.

Put on the armor of God to achieve victory.

Download the daily "Family" readings from www.e625.com/lessons.

The word Philippians derives from the name of the Greek city called Philippi, named after Philip II of Macedonia, the father of Alexander the Great. The city was strategically located as a gateway to Europe. Philippi was the first place in Macedonia in which Paul founded a church, and it became the cradle of Christianity in Europe. It is believed that this letter was written around the year 61 AD, during the time of Paul's imprisonment in Rome. The letter to the church in Philippi is Paul's most personal letter.

Welcome and introductory questions (10 minutes)

Before starting the lesson and after greeting your middle schoolers, take three minutes to ask three non-personal questions, designed to be inviting and unintimidating. These can be directed toward the whole class, or you can call on someone you know will be comfortable answering in front of the whole group:

1. Have you ever told a lie or done something to impress somebody? What?
2. How easy is it to keep up appearances? Why?
3. Who are we fooling when we do things for the sake of appearances?

Paul begins his letter to the Philippians by greeting them with great affection, but he soon mentions some people who are preaching out of envy and rivalry. It seems that even in the time of Paul there were people with twisted hearts, creating an appearance of their own goodness while actually full of rivalry and envy toward others. The movies don't seem to be very original; the Bible already has it all! Read Philippians 1:15-17.

The perfect deception (15-20 minutes)

Divide the group in two, the girls on one side and the boys on the other.
Ask two leaders or volunteers, a man and a woman who are capable of acting, to help you with this skit. You can also use two young people who are spontaneous and funny. The two actors, pencil and paper in hand, will ask the students to tell them what they consider the ideal qualities a girl and a boy should have and write them down: the boys will tell the "actor" the qualities of an ideal girl, and the girls will tell the "actress" what an ideal boy would be like. For example: kind, elegant, like sports, cook well... etc. They can write down about five or six characteristics.

Then let the performance begin! Ask the actors to start a conversation pretending that they like each other and are on a first date, and that they want to impress the other, making sure to demonstrate all the qualities that were dictated to them. They have five minutes or less to represent all the qualities. Once they're done, ask the girls what qualities they think the boys asked for based on the performance, and ask the boy what qualities they think the girls asked for.

We all want to impress others at times, but only what comes from the heart is true and lasting.

In what other situations do we try to impress others?

- When looking for a job.
- When meeting the parents of a significant other.
- With the pastors.
- With the leaders.
- With the school principal or teachers.
- With our friends.
- In sports.

A look at content
Paul tells the Philippians very clearly how to deal with this.

Read Philippians 2:3-4
How should we do things?
How can or should we seek our own benefit?

Read Philippians 2:5-8
How is Christ the perfect example?

Read Philippians 2:9-11
What was His reward?
What happens to those who take on under-the-radar but difficult tasks that very few notice?

Read Philippians 2:13-17
What is Paul's example?
Why do you think he says those people will shine like stars?
Finally, Paul gives a "magic" key that solves everything.

Read Philippians 4:4-8
What is a virtue?
Is practicing this virtue pretending?

We must certainly strive to become more and more like Jesus, but this does not come by pretending or doing anything by our own strength. We become more like Jesus from an intimate communion with the Father, who with His Holy Spirit gives us the desire to fulfill His will. In order to achieve this, we must spend time with God so that His virtues can develop within us. When we spend a lot of time with a person, some of their attributes stick with us and some of our attributes stick with them, too. This will also happen with God. Spending time with Him and trying to get to know Him more will result in God's characteristics rubbing off on us. As Philippians 1:6 says, "He who began a good work in you will carry it on to completion until the day of Christ Jesus."

Download the daily "Family" readings from www.e625.com/lessons.

Paul wrote this letter to the church that was meeting at Colossae (modern Turkey), with the suggestion that it be shared with their neighbors at the church in Laodicea. The church was growing, and false doctrines were an imminent threat. There were issues with rituals surrounding food, human traditions, and false philosophies. Paul's concern for his people makes the central objective of the letter evident: Jesus Christ is God, and His sacrifice on the cross refocuses our lives toward fullness in Him.

Welcome and introductory questions (10 minutes)

Before starting the lesson and after greeting your middle schoolers, take three minutes to ask three non-personal questions, designed to be inviting and unintimidating. These can be directed toward the whole class, or you can call on someone you know will be comfortable answering in front of the whole group:

1. If you had to define who Christ is in a short sentence, what would you say?
2. Thinking about specific things for everyday life, how is life different with or without Christ?
3. Do you think it is preferable to live with Christ or without Christ? Why?

Colossians is a fairly short letter, but it has lots of content. We could divide it into two large sections. The first one tells us who Christ is. The second one tells us who we are, individually and as a community, when we resurrect with Him to a new life. The book goes back and forth between things that seem very spiritual and their practical consequences in our lives. One thing is clear: with Christ, things are different. It is in Christ that our nature is changed and, as a consequence, our behavior and our entire way of living is transformed.

Main ideas (30 minutes)

Divide your group into four smaller groups (or two, depending on the number of students you have). You can do it as follows: stick posters labeled with the numbers 1, 2, 3, and 4 in four corners of the room, one in each corner. If you only have two groups, or if your group is not very large, you do not need to do this step.

Prepare in advance squares of paper in four colors, and write the numbers one through four on each piece of paper, regardless of color. Then put them face down so that the number cannot be seen, with the papers separated by color. Students might think you'll be dividing groups by color, but when they turn the paper they will find a number, and that will be their team. Keep in mind that you must have the correct amount of numbers and colors for the number of students you have.

If you want, you can add one more step and prepare four special papers, one in each color, that say "leader." The four students who end up with a "leader" paper will guide their team in the activity.

Colossians has four chapters (hence the four teams). Print the four chapters separately, one for each team, so they can mark it up. You may need several copies of each chapter depending on the amount of participants. Ideally you can make one copy for every two students to share. Give students four markers to underline the different words below. Have students find how many times in the chapter the following words (or those related to them) are mentioned:

- Knowledge and wisdom (know, learn, etc.).
- Fulfillment (full, complete).
- Body (individual or community).
- Christ (Jesus Christ, God, Lord, etc.).

What important ideas are related to these words?

Complete the picture with the proclamations about Christ given by Paul to the Colossians.

The Complete Picture
Complete the picture with Paul's statements to the Colossians about Christ. The tables that follow are complete. Download and print a chart for each team in the complimentary material section at the link below.

Download from www.e625.com/lessons the complimentary materials for this section

Book overview (10 minutes)
Paul appears to be repetitive with some concepts. He obviously doesn't want any doubts to remain. Let's look together at some of the many things he states.

Wisdom
In all of human history there has never been a time in which people have had the level of access to information we have today. We search online and with a simple tutorial we can learn anything, from how to bake a chocolate cake to how to assemble a nuclear bomb. However, our daily reality clearly shows us that this is not exactly the wisest era we've ever lived through. We know more than ever about medicine, but our mortality rates have increased. We produce food more efficiently than ever,

but there are still people without food on their table. We can be connected online 24 hours a day, but achieving an authentic connection with others seems like mission impossible.

"For this reason, since the day we heard about you, we have not stopped praying for you. We continually ask God to fill you with the knowledge of his will through all the wisdom and understanding that the Spirit gives, so that you may live a life worthy of the Lord and please him in every way: bearing fruit in every good work, growing in the knowledge of God, being strengthened with all power according to his glorious might so that you may have great endurance and patience, and giving joyful thanks to the Father, who has qualified you to share in the inheritance of his holy people in the kingdom of light" (Col 1:9-12).

Identity

In the chart that you put together earlier, we could clearly see some statements about the identity of Christ and about our own identity in Him. Middle school is a stage in your life when you likely have many questions. Who am I, really? Who do I want to be? What do I want to do?

Our society constantly associates fulfillment with material things. It can seem like the more material things you have, the more fulfilled you will be. However, the fulfillment God promises is much greater: It defines who we are when we die to our life without Him, and we instead dare to follow Him. It allows us to build a new identity based on the purpose our Creator had when He planned our lives, an identity that's much more valuable, useful, and desirable (Ps. 139:13-16).

Body

Being in Christ changes your life. Not only that, it changes the larger community of faith. The evolution of society has led us to see life in an increasingly individualistic way. But humans can't live without one another. We are vulnerable, we need each other, and we cannot (nor do we want to) be alone.

The church IS the body of Christ. It is the way in which He manifests Himself, speaks to us, and cares for us. Without that community, we cannot be fulfilled. Beyond the difficult situations you may face in school, at home, or in your neighborhood, it is important that you find your place in this body of Christ, which not only wants to receive you and accompany you, but in which there is a place for you and for your gifts that no one else can replace (Eph. 4:15-16).

Closing

Choose a song that focuses on Jesus and invite your students to reflect on the lyrics. Then sing it together.

Dare to seek the things from above. Christ is enough.

Download the daily "Family" readings from www.e625.com/lessons.

The recipient of this letter is Philemon, one of the most important members of the church in Colossae. The letter is also addressed to his family and to the church that met in his house. Philemon had come to know the Lord through Paul. He had some slaves, and one of them, Onesimus, ran away from his master. Somehow he came to know Paul and, through Paul, the message of salvation. Then Paul sent Onesimus back to his master, but with this letter of recommendation so that not only would he be accepted back by Philemon and not executed, but he would also be recognized as a brother in Christ. This letter represents the strength of God's love in us. By receiving forgiveness and mercy from Him, we can in turn give to others with compassion.

Main doctrines:

Forgiveness: Christ offers the perfect example of forgiveness (Phil. 1:16-17; Mt. 6:12-15; 18:21-35; Eph. 4:32; and Col. 3:13).

Equality: Christianity ended the evil of slavery by changing the hearts of slave owners and the enslaved, emphasizing the spiritual equality of both (Phil. 1:16; Mt. 20:1-16; Mark 10:31; Gal. 3:28, Eph. 6:9; Col. 4:1; 1 Tim. 6:1-2).

Welcome and introductory questions (10 minutes)

Before starting the lesson and after greeting your middle schoolers, take three minutes to ask three non-personal questions, designed to be inviting and unintimidating. These can be directed toward the whole class, or you can call on someone you know will be comfortable answering in front of the whole group:

1. What are the most difficult things to forgive?
2. What is the most difficult thing you have had to forgive? How did you show you had forgiven (actions, words, etc.)?
3. What is the hardest thing that you have had to ask forgiveness for? Why was it so difficult? What were the consequences?

It is very difficult for all of us to forgive and love again. It is also very difficult to ask for forgiveness from the heart, accepting the consequences of what we've done wrong. But asking for forgiveness and forgiving is the example that Jesus himself left for us by sacrificing Himself for what we had done wrong. It is difficult for us to obey, but when we do, good things happen. Loving God means obeying His commandments (John 5:3). One of His commandments is to love our neighbors as ourselves (Mt. 22:39).

Many times we have to forgive without having been asked for forgiveness. We often have to love without pretending—truly love—even at a cost to ourselves (Rom. 12:9-10). All this boils down to the fact that we can choose to love and we can choose to forgive, but we need to act from the heart.

Taboo! (20 minutes)

This game requires you to divide the group into two or more teams. You can do this in the following way: first ask students to divide into boys and girls. Then, depending on the size of your group, you can stay with those two teams, or you can subdivide them into two more teams by grade, by age, or by numbering them.

A- Paper option

Four posters will be needed. On each poster, write a TABOO word (the word that the participants have to guess) and its prohibited words (which are usually synonyms or antonyms of the main word).

One volunteer from each team will come forward, all four at the same time. Without those four volunteers seeing the word, show the first word to the rest of the players in the audience. Each group, at the same time, must give clues to their player so that they can guess the word before the other teams. The rule is that no related word, either synonyms or antonyms, can be mentioned. You can use just the four words listed below, or add more depending on the time you have. You will also need someone to help you check that students do not cheat. The player who writes the correct word first wins the point.

The posters are:
1. Love
Forbidden words:
- Affection
- Tenderness
- Fondness
- Hatred

2. Forgiveness
Forbidden words:
- Love
- Liberation
- Cross
- Apology
- Request
- Retraction

3. Obedience
Forbidden words:
- Disobedience
- Discipline
- Authority
- Allegiance

4.Equality
Forbidden words:
- Inequality
- Equal
- Inclusion
- Equivalence
- Equity
- Other

B- Technological option
At the beginning of class the teacher should get everyone's cell phone number. Create a text chain so that all participants can communicate. You must make sure that those going to the front do not take their cell phones with them. With this option, text the word by message to everyone, or to one in each group. Then the game will play out as explained above.

This text thread can also be used to communicate with students during the week—to send them Bible verses, and ask them how they are doing and how their week is going.

Book overview (20 minutes)
Hide pieces of paper under the students' chairs that have printed on them the following biblical quotes. The book of Philemon is short and simple (it only has one chapter) so it can be divided into four parts.

1. Greeting: Philemon 1:1-3
2. The virtue of one who forgives: Philemon 1:4-7
3. The actions of one who forgives: Philemon 1:8-18
4. The motives of one who forgives: Philemon 1:19-25

Paul was in prison for Christ. Somehow, he met Onesimus, who had converted to Christianity. Onesimus was a slave, owned by Philemon. He had stolen from Philemon and run away. Roman laws said that any slave who ran away from his master must be sent back to his master's home, who would then most likely punish him severely and could even execute him. Although Onesimus was very useful to Paul, Paul made the right decision to send Onesimus back to Philemon. But he did not send him empty-handed: Paul wrote this letter, which fully discusses true forgiveness.

1. v. 1-7 What is the best way to begin when you want to ask for something from someone? Especially from your dad and mom. Yes! Recognizing the good in people, valuing their effort and work, and highlighting their qualities. These things help to prepare the moment.

2. v. 8-10 Why does Paul say that he could order it, but he prefers to ask for it out of love?

We are probably used to being given orders when asked to do things, perhaps because that is the only way we will do them. To ask out of love is a risk, because the other person could say no. Onesimus had become a spiritual son of Paul. In one ·of their conversations, Onesimus must have told Paul who his master was and what had happened, and how he regretted what he had done (although the letter does not specify this). So Paul and Onesimus decide to act with responsibility and love. This would be a good lesson for both the master and the slave.

Speaking of slaves, at the time of the early church, it wasn't unusual to be a slave or to have slaves, but Christianity not only came to free the souls of believers, but also to free them from physical chains. Have you ever experienced contempt? Have you seen someone treat another person with contempt? Have you seen someone enslaved to another person? There are many ways to be a slave. You can be a slave over debts, favors, work, social position, or over being friends with someone popular. But Jesus came to teach us to be free, to choose to live for Christ.

3 v. 11-19 How does Paul ask that Onesimus be received by Philemon?

Obviously something had happened between Onesimus and Philemon, leading Onesimus to escape. Now Onesimus understood what he needed to do: Return to his master and ask for his forgiveness. Paul asks even more of Philemon. To forgive Onesimus and to receive him as a brother, even as he would receive Paul himself. Of course, Onesimus had been a bad servant and Paul was a respected character. Paul asks for a lot, because he understands who Onesimus is now and how much he has changed. So much so that Paul even offers to pay any debt Onesimus has with Philemon (although at this point Paul reminds Philemon of how much he owes him... good strategy).

4.v. 20-22 What is Paul's expectation?
Paul not only asks him for everything we mentioned, but he closes with, "I am sure that you will do what I ask of you and much more." What will that much more be?

Closing (10 minutes)

Forgive and ask for forgiveness: Download and print a copy of the following sheet for each student. Or, you can ask them to close their eyes and ask themselves these questions for reflection, without answering out loud.

1. What is more difficult, to forgive or to ask for forgiveness? Why?
2. Can I recall what another person did to me again once I forgive them? Why?
3. How do we show true forgiveness?
4. Can we forgive without being asked for forgiveness? Why?
5. Is there something for which you should have asked for forgiveness for but never did? What was it, and who should you have asked?

Download the daily "Family" readings from www.e625.com/lessons.

Then ask them to open their eyes and conclude with this: Although slavery was allowed, the message of salvation was for everyone, and when a slave converted to Christ he also became a brother in Christ, equal to his masters in Jesus' eyes.
The forgiveness Paul is teaching has nothing to do with rules, debt, or repentance. It has to do with becoming just like Jesus, who, whether we deserved it or not, whether we owed a large debt or not, was merciful to us. We were less than slaves, but Jesus sent us to the Father with a letter written in blood, stating that He had paid for our sins, that He had redeemed us from any debt we owed to our Master.

We don't know what happened to Philemon. He likely never saw Paul again, but if he did what Paul begged of him, he surely gained a faithful friend for life.
Forgiving and asking for forgiveness are two different sides of the same coin. Forgiving is difficult because if we forgive we have to do it just like Jesus did: out of love, with mercy and as restoration. If we attempt to "forget it" but still remember what was done to us all the time and keep reminding that person about it, then it wasn't forgiveness.

The Father broke once and for all the curse of sin. Every time He looks at us, He does not see who we were, but instead sees the blood of Jesus. We have to learn to forgive in that same way.

On the other hand, asking for forgiveness is difficult because it means being repentant, changing our attitude, and putting ourselves in the hands of the one who can forgive us. If this person knows the Lord, he will possibly know how to forgive us like Him, but if he doesn't, we have to be willing to correct our mistakes and suffer the consequences.

Forgiving offenses not only restores our relationships and breaks the chains of those who ask for forgiveness, it also frees us to love without anger and without bitterness. It sets us free.

Close with a prayer, asking the Lord to forgive us for our offenses against Him, making a prayer of faith and surrender to give the opportunity to those who have not done it yet. Also asks the Holy Spirit to remind students if they should ask for forgiveness from someone they have offended, or if they need to forgive someone in order to be free. Send them away in the name of the Lord.

Download the daily "Family" readings from www.e625.com/lessons.

The apostle Paul was a great maker of disciples. During his time as an apostle he made many disciples who accompanied him on his missionary journeys and in his time in prison, and who he also trained in their ministries. Among the 14 letters of Paul in the Bible, only four letters are to individuals. These letters to his children in the faith are known as "the pastoral epistles." We will now focus on Paul's first letter to Timothy and his letter to Titus.

Both letters were written by Paul after he was released from house arrest in Rome, and before he was imprisoned again and executed. Paul had left Timothy in charge of the church in Ephesus and Titus in charge of the church in Crete. He wrote to them to strengthen their ministry and to encourage them, since they were both very young. Paul did not talk about Christian doctrine in these letters because his disciples knew it very well. Instead, he wanted to encourage them to continue with the work, and to give them some advice so that things would go well.

Welcome and introductory questions (10 minutes)

Before starting the lesson and after greeting your middle schoolers, take three minutes to ask three non-personal questions, designed to be inviting and unintimidating. These can be directed toward the whole class, or you can call on someone you know will be comfortable answering in front of the whole group:œ

1. How old does someone need to be to have a job? Why?
2. What are some of the duties of church leaders and pastors?
3. How old does someone need to be to become a leader in the church?

We're going to look at the first letter the apostle Paul wrote to Timothy and his letter to Titus. Both Titus and Timothy were young men who were each in charge of a church. Timothy in the city of Ephesus (1 Tim. 4:12) and Titus of the church at Crete (Ti. 1:4 and 5). The fact that they were young was not an impediment. On the contrary! Paul told Timothy to be an example in everything, in the way he spoke, in his conduct, in love, in faith, and in purity.

It is great when we can have a relationship with the Lord Jesus from a very young age. Throughout our lives we can allow Him to help us make a difference with our actions, making what we think, say, and do meaningful.
Would you like to become a leader at your local church? What can we do to be young people like Timothy and Titus, capable of being entrusted with the task of leading a church?

Game: Telephone (20 minutes)

Divide the group into two or more teams depending on the number of students. Divide them as follows: Choose two or more captains. Prepare as many cards as teams you need to make. Each card will be a different color on one side, but the same color on the other (playing cards can work for this).

Designate a color for each captain. Then each player, without seeing the team colors, must choose a card. Then have them look at their card and join the team of the color they received. Mix the cards up as each student makes a selection. Once a team reaches its capacity, remove that color of card. When all the teams are chosen, have students line up in rows to play telephone. Try to mix them by gender, boy-girl-boy-girl.

Give the team captain a piece of paper with the messages you have chosen to pass. At your command, they will whisper the message quietly into the ear of their first teammate, then from that teammate to the next and so on until they reach the last person, who will have a paper and pencil. That last person should write down the message they heard. The team that passes the message the fastest and closest to the original text is the winner. Choose three messages to pass on per team.

Messages to pass on:
Some of these messages were paraphrased to make them shorter. You can use some or all of them, depending on the time that you have.
> 1 Tim. 1:5: "...let love be of a pure heart, a good conscience, and sincere faith."
> 1 Tim. 2:1; Titus 3:1: "...make prayers, supplications and thanksgiving for all."
> 1 Tim. 2:11; Titus 3:2: "...lift your hands to heaven with purity of heart, without anger or strife."
> 1 Tim. 3:2; Titus 1:8: "...be blameless, temperate, sensible, respectable, hospitable, able to teach."
> 1 Tim. 3:3; Titus 1:7: "...not a drunkard or a brawler, nor a lover of money, but kind and peaceful."
> 1 Tim. 4:8; Titus 2:12: "…godliness is useful for everything, since it includes a promise for eternity."
> 1 Tim. 4:12; Titus 2:7: "...may they see in you an example to follow, how to speak, in conduct, in love, faith and purity."
> 1 Tim. 4:13; Titus 2:1: "...devote yourself to the public reading of the Scriptures, and to teaching and encouraging the brethren."
> 1 Tim. 4:16: "Be careful of your conduct and your teaching."
> 1 Tim. 6:11; Titus 3:14: "Make every effort to pursue righteousness, godliness, faith, love, perseverance and humility."
> Titus 3:13: "Help others as much as you can."

Titus 3:14; 1 Tim 6:12: "pay attention to what's really necessary and do not lead a useless life."

Message in Paul's letters (10-15 minutes)

When messages are passed on from one person to another, they often become distorted. Many times we repeat something we hear, and it ends up hurting people and harming our relationship with our brothers and sisters and with God. At the time these books of the Bible were written, some people in the church were sending the wrong message. Paul sent his disciples to help these churches correct their understanding.

Either ask a student to read the following verses, put them on a poster and have everyone read them together, or recite them yourself.

In the letter to Titus Paul says: "At one time we too were foolish, disobedient, deceived and enslaved by all kinds of passions and pleasures. We lived in malice and envy, being hated and hating one another" (Titus 3:3).

Paul had been a Torah scholar since his birth. He had been passionate about fulfilling the law as he understood it. But when he learned the message of salvation, he rethought his past behavior.

In Timothy Paul says, "We also know that the law is made not for the righteous but for lawbreakers and rebels, the ungodly and sinful, the unholy and irreligious, for those who kill their fathers or mothers, for murderers" (1 Tim. 1:9).

The law is necessary for those who don't know God's love. Those who do not know Christ can only be governed by the law and what it demands. But before the time of Jesus, God's law was extremely rigid, no one could fulfill it, and we all deserved death. Until Jesus came.

Titus 3:3-8: "At one time we too were foolish, disobedient, deceived and enslaved by all kinds of passions and pleasures. We lived in malice and envy, being hated and hating one another. But when the kindness and love of God our Savior appeared, he saved us, not because of righteous things we had done, but because of his mercy. He saved us through the washing of rebirth and renewal by the Holy Spirit, whom he poured out on us generously through Jesus Christ our Savior, so that, having been justified by his grace, we might become heirs having the hope of eternal life. This is a trustworthy saying. And I want you to stress these things, so that those who have trusted in God may be careful to devote themselves to doing what is good. These things are excellent and profitable for everyone."

Jesus died unjustly, having no sin, and in doing this He paid for all of us. He fulfilled the whole law, and in that way He made us righteous. Then by grace we gained eternal life. Now Paul says that knowing this goodness of God, we have nothing left but to do good works, because that is what we learned from God. Act toward others out of grace, which benefits everyone. Paul is giving some clues to Timothy and Titus on how to help the church be a witness, a community in which people not only believe but live as children of God.

It didn't matter that Titus and Timothy were young. It mattered that they loved the Lord and served Him with passion and love. They became leaders for a church that served and loved the Lord and spread His message of salvation.

Closing (10 minutes)

Write on a whiteboard or large poster only the first and last letters of a word or phrase, then add as many blanks as there are missing letters.

Example:
(Sensibility) S_ _ _ _ _ _ _ _ _ y

Players, individually or in teams, will try to guess the hidden letters. They have five chances. If they fail five times, it will be the turn of another player or rival team.

Examples of words to use:
Example.
Friend.
Fairness.
Discipline.
Integrity.
Impeccable.
Grace.

End with a prayer about God's calling for your students. Ask Him to prepare them and put in their minds and hearts any calling or way of serving through which they will be able to develop their gifts.

Download the daily "Family" readings from www.e625.com/lessons.

The name Timothy means "one who honors God." Names are very important, not only to let people know what to call us, but also because name meanings are often related to God. In this case, we are going to see how the apostle Paul reminded Timothy to wear his name well by honoring God. Paul wrote this letter while imprisoned once again in Rome, shortly before being sentenced to death by Nero around the year 67 AD. Paul encouraged Timothy to visit him in Rome before his execution. He also encouraged Timothy to remain faithful in his duties, retain sound doctrine, accept persecution over the gospel, and trust and preach the Scriptures.

In this lesson we will see what advice a "prisoner of Christ" gives to his beloved disciple.

Welcome and introductory questions (10 minutes)

Before starting the lesson and after greeting your middle schoolers, take three minutes to ask three non-personal questions, designed to be inviting and unintimidating. These can be directed toward the whole class, or you can call on someone you know will be comfortable answering in front of the whole group:

In our class about Acts we talked a bit about God calling Paul to take the message "to the ends of the earth." Obviously Paul did not reach all corners of the earth. In fact, it is believed that he died in a prison in Rome a few years after beginning his ministry. Timothy was with Paul and accompanied him on his travels, serving as Paul's messenger on several occasions. He was eventually left in charge of a congregation in the city of Ephesus.

1. What does it mean to be a missionary?
2. What advantages does being a missionary have, and what sacrifices does being a missionary require?
3. What motive or reason might someone have for becoming a missionary?

¿Cuántas veces hemos escuchado testimonios de personas que dejaron sus familiares, sus amigos, su tierra, su lengua y se fueron a otros lugares a compartir el mensaje de salvación? ¡Qué ejemplos de amor y obediencia a Dios!

Have you heard testimonies of people who left their families, their friends, their land, their language, and went to other places to share the message of salvation? What great examples of love and obedience to God!

Paul was a great missionary. He understood that he needed to share the Lord's message of salvation with others. But before Paul met God, Paul used to do the opposite.

Who knows what Paul used to do before he became a believer?
Paul persecuted Christians, searching for and even killing them because he thought Christians were offensive to God. Paul wanted to please God, and he thought persecuting Christians was the way to do it. Paul declares this in the first letter to Timothy in chapter 1:13:

"Even though I was once a blasphemer and a persecutor and a violent man, I was shown mercy because I acted in ignorance and unbelief."

But when God revealed himself to Paul, who back then was Saul, he believed in God (Acts 9). With that same desire to please Him he had shown before, Paul began serving God by preaching Jesus as the Messiah who rescues us from death. Paul became the most important missionary in history, spreading the gospel throughout Europe and Mesopotamia.

In Matthew 28:19-20, Jesus said, *"Therefore go and make disciples of all nations, baptizing them in the name of the Father and of the Son and of the Holy Spirit, and teaching them to obey everything I have commanded you. And surely I am with you always, to the very end of the age."*

This is exactly what the apostle Paul did. Some people receive the call to go to other faraway places, and others do not. But the mission Jesus left to His disciples before ascending to heaven is for all of us. Like Paul, we all must speak of Him and what He did on the cross. Are we doing this? Do we talk to our loved ones, friends, acquaintances, or strangers about the message of salvation through Jesus?

Three pieces of advice for Timothy
Give your students a copy of the "Three pieces of advice from Paul to Timothy" handout. Working in pairs, they must match the verses that talk about the same topic. Whoever finishes first wins. They need to not only complete the task, but be able to explain why they put them together the way that they did.

Download from www.e625.com/lessons the complimentary materials for this section

Reflection:

There is a popular saying: "experience is the best teacher." Paul assures Timothy that he will suffer persecution for following Christ (Read 2 Tim. 1:8 and 2:11-13). Jesus Himself told His disciples that they would have tribulations in the world (John 16:33). Jesus knew well what it was to suffer, and he knew even better what his last and greatest test of persevering was. He knew his disciples would suffer. Paul knew Timothy would suffer as well.

Whenever you are going through a difficult situation, remember what happened to Paul. Remember the Lord's advice. He already knows that life has beautiful moments, but also others that are very difficult.

Surely at some point you must have experienced a situation that hurt you. Maybe you were treated unjustly. Maybe you've lived through grief after losing a loved one. Remember, Jesus was the first to say that difficult things were going to happen to us. That does not mean we should turn our backs on Him. Quite the opposite. We must trust, believe in Him, and wait for Him to act. In fact, the full verse from John says, *"I have told you these things so that in me you may find peace. In this world you are going to suffer, but take heart, I have overcome the world."*

That is why knowing the Word of God is so important. In the Scriptures we find God's will for our lives and can come to know God's heart and His promises. Read 2 Tim. 1:13-14 and 3:14-17. Paul emphasizes important themes for Timothy, and for us, to carry with us.

The Word of the Lord is precious and the Holy Spirit brings it to our minds when we need it, whether to help someone, to communicate the message of salvation, or to find comfort and encouragement. What else do the verses say? Why are the Scriptures important?

2 Tim. 1:13 says, *"Follow the example of sound doctrine."* Why does he call it "sound"? Maybe it's because it's for our own good. And that brings us to the third piece of advice (2 Tim. 1:8-2:13).

What is the life to which the Lord has called us? How can we achieve it? Paul says it is by grace that we achieve holiness, but the way we behave reflects who we are. Through the power of the Holy Spirit we can remain firm in the Word of the Lord and be equipped for all good works. How can we avoid the negative impulses that come with being young and live into our calling as followers of Christ?

Closing (10 minutes)

The Lord has delivered us from evil and died as a sacrifice to make us free. That's why we love Him and persevere. But that's not all: In His Word we find the encouragement and the faith to remain firm in His truth. Everything has been accomplished by the work of Jesus on the cross and not by our strength. Still, we must be wise and avoid exposing ourselves to evil things. We should not tempt God by testing His grace and goodness. We must reflect on our behavior now that we are in Him and change when we are doing things that are not good for us or others. We must become missionaries of Jesus here and now, in our schools, in our neighborhoods, or wherever the Lord takes us.

Take a few minutes to pray for your students. Ask for the wisdom you have focused on today to impact their lives going forward. You can also finish by asking them to write a letter to the Lord responding to these three requests from Paul, confessing their fears, their weaknesses, and their commitment to follow Him.

Download the daily "Family" readings from www.e625.com/lessons.

Peter's first letter begins by identifying its author. Although some doubt that the author Peter, believing the language sounds too sophisticated for a fisherman, this letter is undoubtedly his first inspired writing. It is also believed that Silas helped Peter with the grammar (although Peter had been trained to become the main preacher of the gospel from the day of Pentecost, with the outpouring of the Holy Spirit) (Acts 2-12).

At the time of his writing, Rome was decadent, and Christians were harshly persecuted. This context allows us to better appreciate the message of encouragement and resistance that Peter sends to the church. We first encounter Peter in the Gospels. He was the spokesperson of the apostles and was the one who denied Jesus Christ on the night before the crucifixion, only to later encounter the grace of forgiveness and restoration from the resurrected Jesus Christ.

Welcome and introductory questions (10 minutes)

Before starting the lesson and after greeting your middle schoolers, take three minutes to ask three non-personal questions, designed to be inviting and unintimidating. These can be directed toward the whole class, or you can call on someone you know will be comfortable answering in front of the whole group:

1. What was the most difficult day you ever had? What would be a very difficult day for you now?
2. If you could give yourself a message of encouragement for a tough moment, what would you tell yourself?
3. How would you feel after receiving that encouraging message?

At the time this letter was being written, Nero had set fire to Rome and the city was devastated, not only by the destruction but by the inability to find who had started this immense destruction. The great Roman temples, monuments, idols, and houses had been burned and with these losses came great damage to the people's morale and hope. To avoid the people's anger and revolt, Nero redirected the people's ire and frustration toward the Christians, blaming them for the fire. Then a great persecution of believers began. The Christians, or "pilgrims," as Peter called them, needed encouragement and hope for a glorious future in Christ. Peter's first letter is about Jesus Christ embodying the hope given to us to overcome trials and suffering. In the midst of persecution, Peter had the courage to speak about holiness, the perfect nature of Jesus Christ, and the love between Christ's followers.

Drink this water (15 minutes)

Materials needed:
- One bottle with dirty water (the dirtier it looks the better).
- One sealed bottle with clean water.
- 1 water dropper.
- A water purifier (if you can get one).
- An old shirt.
- Some red permanent markers.
- A bottle of red fabric dye.

Game development:
1. Show students the two bottles of water. Present them as a bottle of water you took from the sewer and a bottle of clean water.
2. Ask a volunteer to take the sealed bottle, open it, and take a sip from it.
3. Transfer a small amount of the dirty water to the bottle that has clean water, using the dropper. Cover it and stir well.
4. Ask the volunteer to drink the water again. (If he dares to do it, don't let him!)

Ask:
- Would they drink from either bottle? Why not?
- Why wouldn't they drink from the bottle that has only a few drops of sewage water in it?
- If we were water bottles, what things would contaminate us and make us undrinkable?

Take the old shirt and write with a red marker things that make us dirty or illustrate sin in our lives. You can also prepare several red markers and ask students to write things that represent sin: lies, deceit, insults, resentment, envy, theft, self-hurt, curses, betrayal, abandonment, abusing others, etc.

When everyone has written something, put the shirt in the red dye (very concentrated) and let it soak for a moment, while you say: "Sin, which began in Eden through the disobedience of Adam as the first man, separated us from God, because He is holy. No matter how well we behave or how much we've been through, there is no way to have communion with God if we are not clean as water that can be drunk.

In the same way that we reject the two bottles, even if one is only a little dirty and the other is completely dirty, God rejects sin. His nature does not allow Him to live with it, and He pushes it aside. That is why Christ's work on the cross was necessary. It cleansed us once and for all so that we could once again have a relationship with God through the blood of Jesus Christ. His blood made it so that our evil could no longer be seen, only Jesus' work of redemption." Read 1 Peter 1:18-20.

1 Peter 2:15-17	Goodness, freedom, God's servants, respect, love, honor.

What does it mean that we are free now? How should we use that freedom? What does God want from us?

1 Peter 2:12	Good example, good things, praise God.
1 Peter 3:8-12	Harmony, sharing, blessing, doing good, the Lord takes care of the righteous.

What does Peter recommend? Why does Peter say we should behave this way?

Christ doesn't have to cleanse us all the time. He does not need to die every day for the things we do wrong. His death was once and for all (1 Peter 3:18).

He purifies our water and makes it drinkable, full of special minerals for our health. But it is precisely because of the enormous love Jesus showed on the cross that we accept this purification. Not to continue getting dirty, but to be able to enjoy from now on the freedom of not being tied to anything that puts us down, humiliates us, saddens us, makes us feel like failures or dirty. Jesus has freed us to live a life full of joy, adventure, communion with God and with our fellow followers of Christ. A life full of love, friendship, and blessings.

Does it mean that everything will be easy and perfect?
Does the Lord promise us that we will never suffer? Why?
Do we have to suffer no matter what? Why?

Closing (5 minutes)
Peter knew well that Christians were going through a very difficult time. They were being persecuted and executed for their faith in Christ Jesus; Peter was suffering these things as well. He knew that there was nothing better than living in Christ—forgiven, full of life, and with a purpose and eternal hope in Jesus. That is why Peter taught his readers to leave their previous ways and instead live in God's love.

Pick up the bottles again. How is the water inside of you? Does it need to be purified by the Lord?

Pick up the red shirt. The price paid at the cross was very high, but the price of living according to the love of God is reasonable and pleasant. We may suffer rejection and ridicule from those who think our way of life is crazy, but seeking the good of others, being patient and kind, and loving God is the best way to enjoy earthly life.

What was the price? What were we rescued from? Who did Christ choose? Only Jesus Christ was able to live our lives without being stained by sin, and thus He was able to repay the Just for the unjust to destroy Satan's plan and free us all from the death in life and eternal death.

Take out the shirt. (The idea is that now it should be all red, and the things that we wrote on it cannot be read anymore. If necessary, prepare another shirt in advance that's very red.) Just as this shirt was dyed with red ink to the point that we can no longer see the bad things that stained it, our sins can no longer be seen by God. He only sees the blood of the Righteous One, Christ who makes us clean.

Through the book (20 minutes)

Distribute the following biblical texts. They can be printed or marked in advance for quick reading. Ask a student, or rotate several, to help you write the key words on a board or sheet of paper as they read the verses. (If you want, you can print the references and have them at hand.)

Read the following verses, one after the other:

Verses	Key words
1 Peter 1:3-5	New life, resurrection, living hope, inheritance, no stains.
1 Peter 1:21-23	Through Christ, faith and hope, purified, born again.
1 Peter 1:13-14	Act with intelligence, hope in Jesus.
1 Peter 2:1-3	Leave evil, salvation, try what's good.

How are we purified?
How is this purification reflected in us?
What should we stay away from? Why?

1 Peter 2:9-10	Family, chosen ones, priests, saints, God bought, from darkness to light, compassion.

Who were we before for God? Who are we now?
What does it mean to go from darkness to light?
Would you return to the darkness after you had lived in the light?

As 1 Peter 3:17 says, it is better to suffer for doing good than for doing evil.

But we must stop returning to the things that contaminate us, so we can become focused on what is true and forever. What do you need to get away from? What is contaminating your mind, your body, and your spirit?

Close in prayer, asking the Lord to cleanse the hearts of those who have not yet asked Him to. Ask for forgiveness of sins, for awareness of those things that contaminate us and that we need to remove from our lives. Give thanks to the Lord that we can know him from an early age and live as examples of love and hope.

Download the daily "Family" readings from www.e625.com/lessons.

Lesson 44 > 2 PETER

Peter's second letter sends a clear message about the false doctrines threatening the true message of the gospel, emphasizing that we should patiently wait for the coming of our Lord Jesus Christ. It is likely that Peter wrote this letter from prison in Rome, where he was later martyred and crucified upside down. This letter was written before Nero died by suicide, approximately in the year 67-68 AD.

Welcome and introductory questions (10 minutes)

Before starting the lesson and after greeting your middle schoolers, take three minutes to ask three non-personal questions, designed to be inviting and unintimidating. These can be directed toward the whole class, or you can call on someone you know will be comfortable answering in front of the whole group:

1. What are choices we can make that other people will pretty much always respect?
2. What are some situations you really don't have a choice in?
3. What is the best thing you ever chose to buy? Why did you decide to buy it?

When you are young, you are not allowed to choose much. Usually parents or adults decide what is best, and you have no choice but to accept their decisions. Now that you are in middle school, you have more choices than you used to. With the ability to choose comes the responsibility to choose well.

Peter's second letter makes it clear that God chose us. Many think that giving their lives to God and following Him was their decision, but in reality God's love and mercy chose us, and He gave us the possibility to respond.

Some people during the time of this letter were teaching things that were incorrect, and even went against the truths that Jesus had taught the apostles. In this letter Paul reminds the people of Jesus' important teachings and of standing firm in their faith.

Chosen (10 minutes)

For this activity you will need the video "Take me home, adopt street dogs."

You can find it at the following link: https://www.youtube.com/watch?v=Ek-7fS3BGmcQ (If you can't find this video you can search for any other short five minute film about choosing between two similar things. In this case it is a girl deciding between two dogs to adopt.) You will also need an audio and video player.

In the lesson study about the first letter of Peter it was made clear to us that God has a specific purpose for us. That purpose is why he chose us with love and mercy (1 Pet. 2:9-10). Now he affirms it again (2 Pet. 1:10).

God can do anything—but He chose that today you and I would be sitting here learning about His love. Of course the decision to follow and obey Him is yours, but it starts not with you choosing Him, but Him choosing you. That is incredible! God chooses us because He loves us, and He lets us respond to His love.

The girl in the video chose one of the dogs, and it responded with enthusiasm and acceptance. Sometimes we are like the poodle, reacting to God's choice with rejection. But that will not stop Him from waiting for us and coming back for us. Accepting God's love with enthusiasm is the first step. When we do this, everything around us changes.

When studying the first letter of Peter we learned about the great sacrifice of Christ on the cross, and the inheritance of salvation through Him. We also talked about not going back to our previous behavior, but behaving as who we now are, children of God.

In 2 Peter this truth is reaffirmed.

Read 2 Peter 1:3-8.
Distribute the six verses printed on pieces of paper or already marked in the Bible so that students can participate in the reading.

Read Acts 1:3.
What is a godly life?
What was granted to us to be able to live a godly life?
Why do we want to live our lives this way?

Teacher's Answer Guide
-A godly life is the one that Peter was talking about in his first letter. In harmony, with love, doing good, enduring injustice.
-In order to live a godly life, when we received Christ and accepted His Lordship the Holy Spirit was granted to us.
-Because it is the best way to live. It's what we were created for. Who would not want to live in harmony and freedom in order to do good and receive good?

Read Acts 1:4.

What promises has God given us?
What is God's divine nature?
Is there a way to live in it?

Teacher's Answer Guide
-First, forgiveness and redemption. Freedom. To make us His children. To be our Father. To give us the Holy Spirit to empower us to be His witnesses. Eternal life, etc.
-His nature is perfect love, as is everything it encompasses.
-Yes, through the Holy Spirit, being aware of who we now are in Jesus, and staying in close communion with the Father.

Read Acts 1:5-7.
How does Peter say we should strive?
Does this cycle have a reason?

Teacher's Answer Guide
-Strive to add good conduct to faith. To good conduct, add understanding. To understanding, self-control. To self-control, patience. To patience, devotion to God. To devotion to God, brotherly affection. To brotherly affection, love.
-When we add good conduct to faith, not only stopping from doing the things that contaminate us, but also doing good works just like Jesus did, we will understand the teachings of Jesus and we will grow in our knowledge and understanding of His power. When this happens, it will become easy to have self-control because we will understand what is really important and valuable, and temptation will not be the same. Self-control produces patience, increasing it to the extent that we grow closer in our relationship with the Father. By loving God and spending time with Him, by serving our brothers and sisters with good works, we will develop an affection for others, and that affection will grow into love, which is God's essence.

Read Acts 1:8-9.
What is the end result, or end of that cycle?
What does it mean to be fruitful?
How can we be useful?
What happens to those who do not work on these virtues?

Teacher's Answer Guide
The result is that we'll grow and know the Lord even more, which will trigger the cycle again because by knowing Him more, we will increase our faith, and this will produce more good works, and the cycle will then repeat.

Who wouldn't want to have the best personality? To be the kindest, nicest, friendliest, most understanding, most generous person... etc.? It is impossible to choose otherwise.

Peter's second letter is also about being alert to false teachings that disguise themselves as good, but in reality bring us destruction (2 Pet. 2:1-3, 18-19).

Searching for the truth (20 minutes)

Ask three students to come forward. Explain to them (without the others hearing) that they should think of something extraordinary that they have done. Only one of them will be telling the truth; the other two will invent a story.

Note: If you want you can prepare this in advance with leaders. The truth must be incredible and the lies must be believable!

The purpose of the game is to determine which of the three stories is the truth. Students can ask each participant three questions and then vote on which is true and which is a lie.

When we really know someone, it is very easy to tell when they are lying about themselves.. When Peter was alive there were people who wanted to lie to benefit from the faith. Peter encouraged the church to get to know the Scripture well so that they would not be lost. 2 Peter is a strong call against those lies.

What are lies we hear every day?
That God does not exist because there is suffering.
That you have to listen to your heart (impulses) and not think about the consequences so much.
That you have to live in the moment.
That it is useless to be good to others, and we must seek only our own good.
That it is better to receive than to give.
That only the rich should give to others.
That the injustices we suffer are other people's fault.
That making an effort is not worth it.

Note: Think about situations in your country and in your group to highlight the lies your students hear most.

Most of the "false prophets" of our times are not specific people, but messages that are propagated. We sometimes hear them at home, among our friends, and possibly at church. That's why Peter wrote a whole letter (at a time when it was very difficult to write and send letters) to give a warning about the false teachings that went against God's truth (2 Pet. 3:17-18).

If the principles of the things you hear, see, or read are not reflected in these teachings from Peter, you must discard them before they take up residence in your mind and heart.

Closing (5 minutes)

We must remember these three things every day:

1. We are chosen by God, out of love and grace, not because we deserve it.
2. We must work on our virtues to be strong in Him.
3. We must be smart about the messages we receive daily.

If every day we remember who we are, what we are here for, and what things lift us up versus what things destroy us, we will be winners every day of our lives.

Close in prayer, thanking God for giving us our identity in Him, and for giving us the freedom and ability to respond to Him out of love and gratitude for His sacrifice.

Then ask for the Lord's blessing so that every day your students can remember who they are in Christ and what their mission is. Also ask for protection from the attacks of the evil one.

Note: If you have time you can put together a craft with these three principles, or a poster that you can display in the room where you meet.

Download the daily "Family" readings from www.e625.com/lessons.

Jude, one of Jesus' four half-brothers, wrote this letter before the destruction of Jerusalem in 70 AD. 2 Peter warns of the arrival of false prophets, but Judas is dealing with their actual arrival. Only 25 verses were enough for the author to express the message he wanted to give: to beg Christians to continue fighting vigorously for the faith that was entrusted to them. Jude wrote this book with one theme in mind: salvation. In a short and direct letter, he warns followers of Christ about hidden dangers, and offers tips to help them avoid missing the mark.

Welcome and introductory questions (10 minutes)

Before starting the lesson and after greeting your middle schoolers, take three minutes to ask three non-personal questions, designed to be inviting and unintimidating. These can be directed toward the whole class, or you can call on someone you know will be comfortable answering in front of the whole group:

1. What is the difference between freedom and debauchery?
2. How can the misuse of our freedom affect people? The church?
3. What does compassion mean? Do you remember a moment in which you felt compassion?

In Peter's second letter he warned that false prophets would try to deceive us with false teachings. In this letter, Jude teaches us how to deal with false teachers who, having infiltrated among us, twist the truths of the gospel to confuse Christians new to the faith.

My dictionary (15 minutes)

In Peter's second letter he warned that false prophets would try to deceive us with false teachings. In this letter, Jude teaches us how to deal with false teachers who, having infiltrated among us, twist the truths of the gospel to confuse Christians new to the faith.

Prepare in advance some cards labeled with uncommon words from the dictionary, or use the ones we prepared as examples.

Give each participant a sheet of paper. Each student must invent a definition of the word, trying to use vocabulary to make it sound like a real dictionary definition. Say the word out loud and all students will write their definition.

When they finish writing their definitions, have them turn them in. Read students' definitions along with the true definition.

Together they must decide which definition is true.

If you have many students you can divide them into groups of three or four, with each group collaborating on one definition.

If you don't have much time, you can use the examples we give and let students vote.

EXAMPLES: The definitions in bold are correct.

Dirge	• A carefree community associated with the hippie movement. • **A lament for the dead.** • A shovel used in ancient gardening.
Makebate	• Clumsy person who has difficulty understanding things. • **One that excites contention and quarrels.** • Related to fishing in 19th century England.
Filipendulous	• Having the appearance of an owl. • **Suspended or strung upon a thread.** • Vault-shaped.

Many times we allow ourselves to be fooled by eloquent speech, or by the confidence level of the person we are listening to. Other times we have been taught that respect for our leaders means that we must accept as truth everything they say. But by doing so instead of honoring God, we end up putting our faith in people and not in the truth. The letter of Jude is a clear warning against false teachings that filter into the church and cause us to doubt or stray from the truth.

The three tips given by Jude.
1 - Grace or debauchery.
The fight between grace and debauchery has existed since the earliest times. Paul warns about this in several of his letters, exhorting us not to fall into the temptation that allows so-called freedom to make us take our eyes away from Christ. Jude points out the same risks.

Read Jude 1:4: What were they teaching? What is the difference between the goodness of God and the sovereignty of Jesus Christ?

One of the most wonderful promises of Christ is the call to freedom. *"If you remain in my word, you will truly be my disciples, and you will know the truth, and the truth will set you free"* (John 8:31-32).

But there are two keys to freedom. One is to be His disciple, to follow Him, to learn from Him, and to imitate Him. And the second one is to know the truth. Whoever does not know the truth lives under deception in a parallel reality.

God has given us freedom from sin, which makes us prisoners. He gave us the freedom to have full communion with Him. With His essence of love He also gives us His Holy Spirit, so that we have no choice but to become more and more like Him.

2 - Instincts and passions.

In the previous lesson we talked a little about this. What lies do we hear every day? "Do as you feel," "follow your heart," "if it works for you, go for it!" and so many other phrases we hear on TV, in ads, or in the form of advice from friends. It's common for people to seek their own short term good, not thinking about others or the consequences of their actions.

Read Jude 1:10. Have you ever wished something bad for someone close to you? What would have happened if you had acted on instinct without thinking about the consequences?

It is necessary to oppose injustice, support the rights of innocent people, denounce abusers, etc. None of these things are irrational actions. In those cases we should act out of conviction. But too often the best way to preserve a friend, a relationship with a family member, or remain at peace with a teacher is to keep our mouth shut and bear the situation.

There are many things our heart tells us, but if we allow ourselves to follow them without also using our brain, they will destroy us, just as Jude says.

Let us remember what we learned from the letter to Timothy: *"Flee the evil desires of youth and pursue righteousness, faith, love and peace, along with those who call on the Lord out of a pure heart"* (2 Tim. 2:22).

It is interesting that Paul told Timothy to do this along with those who love the Lord. The love and care for others are only possible if we put aside our own preferences, conveniences, and desires. It is by giving that we receive, by forgiving that we obtain forgiveness, and by dying to ourselves that we find true life.

3- Egoism vs. Perseverance.

When we talk about selfishness we always imagine people hoarding for themselves and thinking only about themselves. Unfortunately the local church is not immune from this disease. We preach a God who is love, and that although He is the owner of everything, the Creator of all things, He wants to relate personally with us. We, on the other hand, tend to be very elitist, often believing others are less than us and unwilling to interact with everyone. We need a new generation committed to others, willing to deny ourselves and instead to love as Jesus loved.

Read Jude 1:17-23. How does Jude say we should be? How should we behave toward those who doubt and those who twist the truth? How can we remain firm in the faith? How can we learn to be guided by the Holy Spirit?

What a coincidence that Judas' advice is having the same attitude that Jesus displayed during His time on earth! That should be the advice we follow, fitting with the Bible teaches us about God's character. And that is in direct opposition to selfishness and individualism.

In Matthew 20:26-28 Jesus says, *"Not so with you. Instead, whoever wants to become great among you must be your servant, and whoever wants to be first must be your slave—just as the Son of Man did not come to be served, but to serve, and to give his life as a ransom for many."*

Yes, this is Jesus. Why should we accept human ideas regarding service and treatment of our brethren and non-brethren in the faith? How should our behavior be instead? What would happen if we all served one another? What would this group be like if we treated each other like Jesus treats others?

Closing: The Smoke Seller (10 minutes)

The short film "The Smoke Seller" directed by Jaume Maestro, from Premier Frame, is an excellent tool for this topic.
https://www.youtube.com/watch?v=YNUbbVZnc9o

"Beware of smoke sellers, who want to pass off something that is not as something that is. They will sell you fake prosperity, and easy success. They will pass off bad as good, for their own benefit (v.16). They are like waterless clouds drifting with the wind, trees without fruit, turbulent waves throwing their shamefully dirty foam into the beach, and restless stars heading towards the densest eternal darkness" (v. 12-13).

In Isaiah 5:20 and 24 we are warned, *"Woe to those who call evil good and good evil, who put darkness for light and light for darkness, who put bitter for sweet and sweet for bitter. Therefore, as tongues of fire lick up straw and as dry grass sinks down in the flames, so their roots will decay and their flowers blow away like dust; for they have rejected the law of the Lord Almighty and spurned the word of the Holy One of Israel."*

Just as Peter did, Jude advises us to remain firm in our faith, in the knowledge of the Word, the love of God, and the guidance of the Holy Spirit, so that "we do not allow ourselves to be carried away by their sins."

Download the daily "Family" readings from www.e625.com/lessons.

The author of the book of Hebrews is unknown. Among its possible writers are Paul, Barnabas, Silas, Apollos, Luke, Philip, Priscilla, Aquila, and Clement of Rome. However, there is no clear verdict. Because it mentions Timothy, who had just been released from prison, it is believed that this letter "to the Hebrews" was written between 67-69 AD. It receives the name Hebrews due to its content, so closely related to the life of the Hebrew people and their customs and laws. It is important to have a good idea of the contents of the book of Leviticus to fully understand the message of Hebrews: sacrifices and the priestly function and its symbology are themes that are addressed to show Jesus Christ as the absolute sacrifice, high priest, and king.

Welcome and introductory questions (10 minutes)

Before starting the lesson and after greeting your middle schoolers, take three minutes to ask three non-personal questions, designed to be inviting and unintimidating. These can be directed toward the whole class, or you can call on someone you know will be comfortable answering in front of the whole group:

1. What are things you do for God every day?
2. In which ways do we fail God every day?
3. What things can we do for God that will allow us to enter heaven?

When God created us he made us without sin, and for that reason we were able to be with Him. When we sin, we are no longer worthy of being in His presence. To be at peace with God, human beings offered animal sacrifices. The punishment that we deserved was passed on to the animal, but it was never enough. For this reason, God sent his own Son as the true sacrifice. When Jesus died on the cross, He fully paid our debt. Now it is our turn to accept this sacrifice as the best gift that we can be given. We no longer have to offer any sacrifices. Jesus died once and forever.

Sufficiently good (15 minutes)

You will need: "The Good-O-Meter vs. Grace" video by CentralFilms, (https://youtu.be/_t9ajHFs4x8?si=otOX58Uy7AnuxlHU), audio, and something to project it on. Show the video The Good-O-Meter vs. Grace. Do you think anyone has ever been good enough to be approved on their own?

Why would Jesus choose that one person and not the others?
Jesus Christ has already paid for us! That's the great news Scripture brings us. The

death sentence we had as a result of our sin has been removed. Jesus took care of the payment, and now He offers us eternal life. God knew we would never be able to pay off that debt. Even though we were the ones who failed, He took the initiative to pay it off for us.

Hebrews 9:12 tells us, *"He did not enter by means of the blood of goats and calves; but he entered the Most Holy Place once for all by his own blood, thus obtaining eternal redemption."*

How do you feel about receiving the best gift ever?

Kings and Priests (20 minutes)

You will need: a bag with enough candy for everyone, a copy of the "Kings & Priests" worksheet, two red flags, and two blue flags.

Divide the larger group into two groups. One of the teams will be called "Kings" and the other team will be called "Priests." To do this, place in a bag the same amount of pieces of paper that say "Kings" and "Priests," based on the number of students you have. Then ask one team to stand on one side of the room, and the others on the other side. In the bag place one red paper that says, "Kings & Priests." The person who picks that piece of paper will be on their own third team, which will be called "Kings & Priests."

Download from www.e625.com/lessons the complimentary materials for this section

Give a "Kings & Priests" sheet to each team. Give them five minutes to study all the information.

Once time is up, proceed to read the sentences below and ask, "True or false?" True is the blue flag, false is the red flag. First you must ask the question. On the count of three, the assigned people from each team must raise the flag to answer at the same time. The team that earns the most points is the winner and takes all the candy. The teams without candy will be punished by having to sing a lullaby while dancing.

Here is the gimmick of the game: the "Kings & Priests" team ALWAYS wins a point, because it represents both. So when the Kings team gets it right, you assign one point to Kings and one point to Kings and Priests. Likewise, when Priests wins, the "Kings & Priests" team also receives a point.v

Pregunta: True or False?	Respuesta correcta
The heart beats 1,000 times a day	False. It beats approximately 100,000 times a day.
The howler monkey can be heard from five kilometers away.	True.
Honey is digested better than sugar.	True.
Less than 1% of Americans eat pizza every day.	False. 13% eat pizza on average.
Charles Darwin traveled on a turtle.	True.
The tomato was originally orange.	False. It was yellow.
More than 4,000 types of potatoes grow in Peru.	True.

You can add more questions if you wish.

The idea is that the "Kings" team and the "Priests" team will have less than seven points and the "Kings and Priests" team will have seven points. Then give the prize to the person from the "Kings and Priests" team. But there is a catch: This person has to learn, at some point in the game, that he is going to receive the prize. But after celebrating, and just when the punishment is about to be imposed on the other teams, you will stop everything and he will have to share the prize with everyone. Don't forget to coordinate this with that person.

Reflection:

The only team that can win the prize is Kings & Priests, always. There is no way for Kings or for Priests to win this game, as at some point they will lose a question. The Kings & Priests team will win it every time.

It's time to serve the punishment!

At this moment this person makes them all winners by distributing the sweets among everyone. While they distribute the candy, tell them the following:
Jesus Christ is the only worthy winner. We were all condemned to be punished, just like those who lost the game. But without deserving it, our KING and PRIEST gave us the gift of eternal life. All we need to do is accept it, just as we accepted the candy we were given. The author of Hebrews tells about the gospel of the kingdom of God

in a way the people could understand, using images and Jewish laws. As we have seen in previous classes about the Old Testament, the priests were the ones who offered sacrifices so that the sin of the people would be paid for.

Only the High Priest could pass into the most holy place where the presence of God was. Year after year they had to deliver sacrifices to be accepted by God. But the good news is that Jesus is the High Priest who tore the veil and paid once and for all with a sacrifice He does not need to make again. His blood is enough. But He did not stop there. He shared with us His reward, which is the gift of eternal life and a new relationship with God, face-to-face.

Read Hebrews 9:11-15; 10:12; 7:27-28.

By faith (10 minutes)
Hebrews 10:22-23

Only by faith can we be certain that all this is so and believe in a perfect future in Jesus Christ.

What is faith?

Hebrews 11:1-3

What characters do you recognize in Hebrews 11:4-31?

Abel.
Noah.
Abraham.
Isaac.
Jacob.
Joseph.
Moses.

What stories do you remember about their faith?

Closing (5 minutes)
Although all of them were approved through their faith, none saw the fulfillment of God's promise. In 11:40-12:2 it says, *"God had planned something better for us so that only together with us would they be made perfect.*

Therefore, since we are surrounded by such a great cloud of witnesses, let us throw off everything that hinders and the sin that so easily entangles. And let us run with perseverance the race marked out for us, fixing our eyes on Jesus, the pioneer and perfecter of faith. For the joy set before him he endured the cross, scorning its shame, and sat down at the right hand of the throne of God."
We only need faith to receive the gift of Jesus' sacrifice.

Close in prayer.

Download the daily "Family" readings from www.e625.com/lessons.

The first epistle of John was written by John the apostle. It's the first of three letters he wrote. Since it does not have any recipient information, it is said to be a general epistle. At the time John wrote this epistle, a movement called Gnosticism was being born. This movement denied the incarnation of Jesus Christ, and propagated false doctrines saying salvation came through knowledge and that the body and spirit were separate. Because of this, John decided to write with the authority of a father to warn the church of these false ideas and to encourage them in love. John thus sought to strengthen basic but profound concepts in the church. When we read John in the Gospel of John, First, Second, and Third John, and Revelation, we can see the zeal with which he defended God's supreme plan through the redemptive work of Jesus Christ.

Welcome and introductory questions (20 minutes)

Before starting the lesson and after greeting your middle schoolers, take three minutes to ask three non-personal questions, designed to be inviting and unintimidating. These can be directed toward the whole class, or you can call on someone you know will be comfortable answering in front of the whole group:

1. What is love?
2. Can you see love? Why?
3. How can we show love?

Note: Each time someone gives an answer, make a note on a whiteboard or large poster (or flip chart). At the end, draw a large heart that encloses all the answers.

The first letter of John is about love, because God is love. That love has to be shown, in the same way that we can feel God's love through His forgiveness. Although sometimes those who need our love most are those for whom we feel it the least, God expects us to show our love to others as He showed it to us: unconditionally, not only through emotions, but through our knowledge about Him.

A hidden treasure (10 minutes)

You will need: small chocolates with wrappers, old newspapers, and trash bags. Prepare some bags in advance full of balls made of crumpled newspaper, simulating garbage. Put the chocolates inside some of the paper balls.
Make sure there is at least one chocolate for each attendee in your group and that you put enough balls of newspaper without chocolates to fill the bags well.

Show the group the bag full of "garbage" and ask them what is in there. Look for answers like garbage, waste, rubbish, etc. Then, explain that inside some papers there are wrapped chocolates and that whoever finds them can keep them. When they find them they can't eat them yet.

Once they are done, they will have the chocolates in their hands and there will be papers lying everywhere. Ask those who have found more than one chocolate to share it with those who don't have any.

Questions:
1. If at the beginning all we saw was garbage, what changed to make us keep looking?
2. Look for someone who has more than one chocolate and ask them if it was worth looking in the bag.
3. Ask the whole group: Why didn't they keep the newspaper? Why did they keep the chocolate?

This is a game for us to learn about Jesus Christ's love for us and how He cleanses us from sin. Each ball of paper with chocolate inside represents what we were like before we met Jesus. Ask the group what we were like before Jesus.
You did what Jesus does in our lives. You saw more than a "garbage bag" and decided to search it (1 Jn. 4:9-10).

When we let Jesus Christ come into our lives and cleanse us of sin, it is similar to what you did when you removed that old, wrinkled paper from your delicious chocolates. Now each of you is very happy to have found what you were looking for. That is how Jesus rejoices when we come to Him and allow Him to cleanse us.

1 John 1:9 says, *"If we confess our sins, he is faithful and just to forgive us our sins and to cleanse us from all unrighteousness."*

Puzzle (10 minutes)
You will need: two puzzles that are exactly the same, with 20 or more pieces. Two Ziploc or similar bags. A bag of marshmallows (the prize).
Put each puzzle in a Ziploc bag. Then take a piece from one of the puzzles and place it in the other puzzle's bag.

Divide the group into two like this: look for a female and a male volunteer. Have them each choose one student at a time, always alternating a boy, then a girl, and so on. Give each team a puzzle bag and tell them that they will have three minutes to put the puzzles together. If they finish within the time limit they will receive a prize.

It's very important to say the phrase it that way because the game is not about one team putting it together the fastest, it's about both puzzles being completed on time.

Set the timer. The team that was missing a piece will likely come to you looking for it. Send them back and tell them to look more carefully. Usually, the team that has an extra piece will not mention it until they finish putting their own puzzle together. When that team finishes, let the timer go until it runs out, or until they share that they have the leftover piece.

Reflection (5 minutes)

First scenario: The players on the team with the extra piece kept the opposing team's piece until they finished putting the puzzle together and declared themselves the winners.

Why did they think they won?
When did they realize they had an extra piece?
Why didn't they mention it? Or, why did they only mention it at the end?
How does the team missing a piece feel knowing the other team had the piece they needed?

Review the instructions again, and have the teams reflect on them. Make them aware that you said they had three minutes to put the puzzles together and it was always about the whole group finishing it, and not about one team winning or losing.

Second scenario: The team that had one extra piece identified the piece and quickly returned it, or shared it with the other team.

Why did they decide to hand over the extra piece?
How did they feel when they heard that the other team was missing a piece?
How did they feel when they received the piece that they were missing?

This is a game for us to learn to show love by supporting others.

1 John 3:17-18 and 20-21: Life is not a competition to accumulate things. We must show the love that Jesus Christ gave us when he took our place on the cross by supporting other people.

God gives us things, experiences, and situations to manage. Just as God gave us His Son as a sign of His love, we can show love to others by supporting them during difficult times.

It's not about you putting together your own puzzle first, it's about all of us supporting each other. Love is seeing ourselves as one team and walking together.

Questions to reflect on:
- What is easier, to love God or to love your brother?
- How do we show that we love God?
- How did God show us His love?

Read 1 John 2:6; 3:14-16; 4:7-10.

Closing (5 minutes)

It is not about feeling love, but about loving because God loved us first and taught us to love. If we do not love our neighbor, we are denying God's love and God Himself, because God is love.

What person do you find difficult to love? Why? Do you believe God loves that person? Why then do you have the right not to love or perhaps even hate that person?

God's work is not complete in our lives, but we can ask Him to help us feel His love for those difficult-to-love people. What will be your next step toward living God's love?

Download the daily "Family" readings from www.e625.com/lessons.

The 2 and 3 John are personal letters. Unlike 1 John, which is a general letter, these two letters have specific recipients: 2 John is addressed to a woman and her family, and 3 John is written to John's friend Gaius. Remember that at this time John is elderly. He describes himself as "the elder" and is seeing new false doctrines like Gnosticism appear. These two letters address issues of hospitality: One warns Christians not to entertain false ministers who seek to distort God's truth, and the other speaks about the obligation to welcome us as brothers within the body of Christ. The central theme continues to be love and how we show it through obedience.

Welcome and introductory questions (20 minutes)

Before starting the lesson and after greeting your middle schoolers, take three minutes to ask three non-personal questions, designed to be inviting and unintimidating. These can be directed toward the whole class, or you can call on someone you know will be comfortable answering in front of the whole group:

1. Have you ever welcomed people you didn't know well into your home? How did it happen?
2. Have you ever gone to stay for a few days at someone else's home?
3. What rules are there in your home for people who visit you?

The letters of 2 and 3 John are written to people who are close to John. In them he shows us important aspects about hospitality and love for others, especially for those who are carrying the word of God everywhere and need help. In John's time, when the church was just beginning, it was very common for evangelists to go from city to city preaching. They suffered from persecution and punishment, and it was very comforting to be able to stay for a few days in the house of fellow followers of Christ.

The Picto-letters.
You need:
Two sheets of paper.
Colored markers.
Divide the class into two equal groups. Then tell each group separately, without the other group hearing, what the letter that they will write should be about. The rule is that they must write it without using words: they can use drawings, scribbles, symbols, etc. Allow them to use their imaginations.

Instructions for the first team's letter:
You should warn a friend from school that you heard that a not-so-friendly classmate is planning to do something mean to him during recess. This classmate has a mud "bomb" prepared to launch at him as soon as he sets foot on the playground. You must warn him by leaving a letter on his desk before the bell rings.

Instructions for the second team's letter:
Your parents are not answering their cell phones, which are probably out of battery. You need to leave them a note explaining that you are going to a friend's house to study, that you will have dinner there, and that you need them to pick you up in three hours.

Give students ten minutes to prepare their cards, following the rules. Then allow one team at a time to show their card and have the other team try to interpret it. Afterward, allow the teams to explain their letters.

Reflection
How did you feel writing these letters?
How would you feel if you received these letters? What would you do?

John's second and third letters are very personal. In these letters John writes to the members of a church to talk about love and how we can show it by following the teachings Jesus left to us, including how to help missionaries who were passing through on their way to another city. There were people who did not recognize Jesus as Lord, and who took advantage of the Christians' hospitality. John warns about them.

How would his friends interpret John's letters? How would they know whose teaching was real or fake?

His answer is in 2 John 1:9.

"Anyone who runs ahead and does not continue in the teaching of Christ does not have God; whoever continues in the teaching has both the Father and the Son."

What does it mean that if someone does not continue in the teachings of Christ he does not have God? Why is it seen like this?

It's better with a guide (15 minutes)
You will need: three jars of water, two stuffed animals, three toy cars, and two large handkerchiefs to blindfold contestants. You must first build a path with obstacles with your team. You should place jars of water, stuffed animals, and cars so that they are not easy to avoid.

Choose two volunteers, blindfold them, and place them in front of the obstacles in the starting position. The idea is that they need to make it to the end without being "hit by cars," without "falling into the endless lake," and without being "attacked by ferocious animals." If they succeed, they win a piece of candy. They will get two tries.

First try: First cover the players' eyes and once they are unable to see, move the objects out of the way so they won't get hurt (but without them knowing). Let them walk blindly, and let them realize how difficult or easy it is to try to avoid obstacles. To add excitement you can throw a stuffed animal at them once they are on their way. Let all the other students shout instructions and warnings to them. Uncover their eyes, and they will realize that they managed to get to the other side because you had cleared the path.

Second try: Now choose two other players who will be their guides. The same players will cover their eyes again and now, without moving the objects out of their way this time, the guides will try to guide the blindfolded players so that they can reach the other side. The guides will walk next to the "blind men," but without touching them.

When they reach the end you will give them their prize, the same prize they did not earn on the first try.

Reflection.

Was it easy to walk through the maze blindfolded? Why?
Did it get better once someone told you how to do it?
You were following orders. Was it a good decision to follow them? Why?

2 John 1:6 tells us, *"And this is love: that we walk in obedience to his commands. As you have heard from the beginning, his command is that you walk in love."*

Following directions through the obstacle course allowed them to safely reach the finish line and obtain the prize. Jesus loves us so much that He left us a series of guides for us to follow, and thus reach the end of the road safely, where the eternal prize awaits us. Many times we resist obeying our parents, teachers, and even God himself, but God loves us, and that the way to show Him our love is to obey Him.

His guidance gives us the parameters to live without hurting ourselves. What does it mean to really love God? Give each student a pencil and paper and time to reflect on which is the most difficult of God's commands to obey. Why do they think it is so difficult to obey that particular command or commands? How can they obey even when it is difficult?

Close with a prayer of gratitude to the Lord for His teachings, because they are life for those who keep them. Ask the Father to guide us to make good decisions every day.

Download the daily "Family" readings from www.e625.com/lessons.

Chapters 1 to 5.

Revelation is the last book of the New Testament, and it was written by the same John who wrote the Gospel of John and John's epistles. At the time he wrote Revelation, John was exiled on the island of Patmos and at an advanced age. There, he received a revelation about the end times directly from Jesus Christ. In these first chapters, Jesus appears before John to send a very important message to seven different churches. He also gives John a vision of heaven. The division of the book into two parts is based on the chronology of Revelation. Chapters 1 to 5 are about events that have already happened, while chapters 6 to 22 are about events yet to be fulfilled. When this book was written, the persecution of Christians had probably already begun, and the figure of the martyrs was beginning to appear. Understanding this, it seems the message of Revelation is about comfort and hope. Revelation reflects on the absolute control by God of all times, past, present and future, bringing to all Christians a certainty about God's divine plan, especially to those who were suffering at the end of the first century.

Welcome and introductory questions (10 minutes)

Before starting the lesson and after greeting your middle schoolers, take three minutes to ask three non-personal questions, designed to be inviting and unintimidating. These can be directed toward the whole class, or you can call on someone you know will be comfortable answering in front of the whole group:

1. Who is your favorite superhero? Why?
2. If that superhero were your friend, what favor would you ask of him?
3. What superheroes exist today?

Revelation begins with Jesus Christ as the protagonist. Jesus shows himself in a different way than He had presented himself when He first came to earth. That humble carpenter now appears dressed as a king, displaying His glory and power and with a message that fills us with hope: He is in control of everything.

This is how my Jesus is (15 minutes)

You will need: printed sheets of "This is how Jesus presented himself," and colored pencils or crayons.

Before giving students their papers, ask them to tell you how they would describe Jesus. Allow them to talk for about three minutes.

Then read Revelation 1:12-16.

Distribute a "This is how Jesus presented himself" sheet to each member of the group.

Download from www.e625.com/lessons the complimentary materials for this section

Give them ten minutes to depict every detail of the description.

Reflection (5 minutes)
* Has anyone changed their perception of Jesus? How did it change?
* What did you like the most about the description in Revelation?
* How would you tell your friends about this description of Jesus?

Jesus Christ died, was resurrected, and returned to heaven to prepare a place for us with Him. Because Jesus was obedient to the Father in everything, He was given power over everything. Jesus had already said He would return, and Revelation confirms that He is King. Just as He promised, in Revelation we see that Jesus is determined to fulfill His redemption plan.

You can be sure that He is in control and that He is going to keep His word. At this moment, our Jesus is preparing for His second coming, and He will come with all the power we heard about.

What do you think of our amazing King?

The Architects (10 minutes)
You will need: one sheet of "The Architects" per person.

Download from www.e625.com/lessons the complimentary materials for this section

Give each person pencils and a copy of "The Architects." Tell them it is their job to finish "building" seven churches. For a church to be considered complete it must have: a cross in the bell tower, a bell tower, a door with a window above it, and two windows on the side. Only if they are complete can they be used. Emphasize the importance of having the churches completed, otherwise the owners will not accept them. Give them five minutes to complete and color the sheet.

What would have happened to the churches if we had not completed them?
Which one required more work? Which was closest to completion?
How would you feel if you had not been able to finish one of the churches?
Who is the church? How can a church be incomplete? What are the consequences of having an incomplete church?

God is love. He loves us so much that He wants us to change what we must change and retain what is good so that we can be with Him for eternity. Chapters 2 and 3 of Revelation show us seven letters Jesus Christ sent to the pastors of seven churches. The church is very important to Jesus Christ; it is part of God's plan. Just as you worked to complete the churches in the game, Jesus sent His message to these churches so they would change what they needed to and could receive eternal rewards.

The seven churches (10 minutes)

Divide your students into groups of four or fewer, and give each group a copy of "The Seven Churches." Let everyone look for the answers and fill in the blanks. Designate a leader from each group to distribute the readings so they can find the answers within 10 minutes and discuss them.

Download from www.e625.com/lessons the complimentary materials for this section

What things you read about are still happening today?
What can we do to avoid making those same mistakes?

No matter how many mistakes we make, the Lord has rescued us. One day He will come with all His glory, just as He promised. Our mind is too finite to imagine it. Revelation 4:11 and 5:9-14 declare the song of the saints to the Lord.

Closing (5 minutes)

Revelation reveals to us in many ways who Christ is: The Son of God, the Faithful Witness, the Firstborn, Sovereign over all the kings of the earth, the Alpha and the Omega, the Beginning and the End, the One who is, the One who was, and the One who is to come, the Almighty, the One who was dead but lives forever, the Lion of Judah, and the Lamb who through His sacrifice has the authority to receive title to all the earth and humanity. This same great Lord is our friend, and he has given up everything for us. Who is Jesus for you?

Close in prayer, thanking the Lord for what He has done, for having humbled Himself for us, but also because one day He will come back with glory and splendor. Pray for those who have understood and recognized the power and mercy of God and wish to give their lives to the great King.

Download the daily "Family" readings from www.e625.com/lessons.

Chapters 6 to 22.

Revelation is the last book of the New Testament, and it was written by the same John who wrote John's Gospel and epistles. At the time he wrote Revelation, John was exiled on the island of Patmos and at an advanced age. There he received a revelation about the end times directly from Jesus Christ. In the first chapters, Jesus appears before John to send a very important message to seven different churches. He also gives him a vision of heaven. The division of the book into two parts is based on the chronology of Revelation. Chapters 1 to 5 are about events that have already happened, while chapters 6 to 22 are about events that are yet to be fulfilled. When this book was written, the persecution of Christians had probably already begun, and the figure of the martyrs was beginning to appear. With this knowledge, we can understand that the message of Revelation is comfort and hope. It reflects on the absolute control by God of all times, past, present and future, bringing to all Christians a certainty about God's divine plan, especially those who were suffering at the end of the first century.

Welcome and introductory questions (10 minutes)

Before starting the lesson and after greeting your middle schoolers, take a few minutes to ask three questions. In this case, ask the entire class:

1. What is the best movie ending you can remember?
2. Do you remember any good movies with bad endings? Why?
3. How would you explain to a person from the time of Jesus what a movie is?

Revelation tells us the end of the story that has been developing since Genesis: The great story of redemption and of the restoration of all things.

John received the vision of what will happen at the end of time and documented it for us. The problem is that John did not understand what he was seeing. He had never encountered such creatures, and he didn't have anything to compare to what he was seeing. He couldn't even explain his vision to his friends. It was like trying to explain to someone from the 1800s about the Internet, or smartphones.

Even for us today, Revelation hides some secrets that we cannot understand because it describes our future, as told by someone from the past. However, it is still without a doubt the best ending that we could have dreamed of.

The strange dream of Christopher Columbus (20 minutes)

Divide the group into three teams as follows. Place as many copies as you need of three different monster figures in a bag. Make sure that there is a shape for each student, and that there are equal copies of each monster so the division will be easy. A representative from each of the teams will come forward. Place three pieces of paper face down on a table, showing these three inventions (one on each piece of paper): a smartphone, a bullet train, and a microwave oven. The three volunteers must imagine that they are back at the time of Christopher Columbus (1500 AD).

One at a time, they must pretend that they are Columbus and have dreamed about the item that they got. They must explain to the crew what they saw in the dream, trying to make them understand it.

Remind them that they cannot use modern words. The three teams must try to guess what the item is. The team with the most correct answers wins.

Variant:
If you have more time, you can write down an invention for each student. Then they must walk around the room talking to their classmates trying to discover as many inventions as possible. As was explained before, players can only give descriptions without using contemporary language, and they must never confirm what the item is. They must let the other player write what they think based on their interpretation. Whoever comes up with the most inventions within five minutes wins. Give all the players a paper and pencil to write down the inventions and corresponding players' names.

Reflection:
- What was the most difficult part of this exercise?
- Did the people who were with Columbus understand what he saw in his dream? Why?
- How would you explain these inventions to your best friend?

Chapters 6 to 22 of the book of Revelation have different symbols that describe the way in which God conclusively defeats evil, judges all people from all times, punishes those who did not accept the gift of salvation, and rewards those who repented from their sins and trusted in Jesus Christ.

Neither you nor I were with John to know what he really saw, so a good way to approach Revelation is to focus on the supreme plan, instead of seeking interpretation of its symbols. John was taken to heaven and to the future, and had to use what he knew to be able to explain things he had never seen. If it was difficult for "Columbus" to explain a smartphone, think how difficult it would have been for John to describe the vision of what had not yet happened.

The Final Battle (20 minutes)

You will need the video from the scene "Battle of Helm's Deep" from The Lord of the Rings: The Two Towers, directed by Peter Jackson, distributed by New Line Cinema.

The clip begins from the moment the king is trapped in the castle and has no way out, other than facing an army of thousands. You can find it at this link: https://youtu.be/Z6XicBBN1l4?si=4kHStXaU9fFTqChs

You will also need audio and a projector.

Start by asking a student to read:
Revelation 11:15: *"Then the seventh angel blew his trumpet, and there were loud voices shouting in heaven: 'The world has now become the Kingdom of our Lord and of his Christ, and he will reign forever and ever.'"*

Revelation 17:14: *"They will wage war against the Lamb, but the Lamb will triumph over them because he is Lord of lords and King of kings—and with him will be his called, chosen and faithful followers."*

Then show them the video of "The Battle of Helm's Deep."

Although there are many fantastic movie scenes, Revelation tells of battles where everything is at stake for eternity. Revelation chapters 6 to 20 narrates the way in which God judges evil. In this final scene, the devil fights with all his might to defeat Jesus Christ, but he cannot win, because Jesus Christ has authority over everything.

He has already defeated the devil personally, and now He is coming for what is His.

In the video, they were waiting for a miracle to rescue them, and yet they also endured, resisting and fighting with everything they had. Thus we must resist and fight to live our lives as Jesus Christ has taught us throughout his Word while we wait for His return. Sometimes we will feel discouraged, lost, or defeated, but we can be sure that if He said He would come, He will fulfill His promise. Everything God has promised He has fulfilled. We have learned this truth throughout all the Bible lessons we have studied.

New heaven, new earth (10 minutes)

Show the photos of "Amazing Buildings" quickly, mentioning what they are called and where they are located. You can download and print them from the complimentary materials at the link below.

Download from www.e625.com/lessons the complimentary materials for this section

Why are all these buildings so magnificent?
Did you know that God is thinking of a design for a mega city for all of us to live in?

If humans can have this amazing creativity, imagine what God can do for us!

Revelation 21:10-12 says, *"And he carried me away in the Spirit to a mountain great and high, and showed me the Holy City, Jerusalem, coming down out of heaven from God. It shone with the glory of God, and its brilliance was like that of a very precious jewel, like a jasper, clear as crystal. It had a great, high wall with twelve gates, and with twelve angels at the gates. On the gates were written the names of the twelve tribes of Israel."*

(Tell them additional details, making sure to read these two passages, describing the materials and other elements in detail. Don't forget to show a lot of emotion.)
At the end of all of history, God has a place prepared for us. That's what Jesus told us in John 14:1-4: that He would go and prepare a place for us. That is what He tells us again in the last two chapters of Revelations (Rev. 21). How exciting!

That's why it's not surprising that John ended the book by writing, "Come!" (Rev. 22:17). Because the coming of Jesus Christ is a great gain for all of us who trust in Him. That is why we do not fear, but instead are full of hope.

Closing (5 minutes)

From start to finish, from creation to the end (which has not yet arrived), God has shown us His love, His mercy, what makes Him angry, what He is capable of doing for us, how He won us back, His plan for us, and His happy ending to this whole great story that is life. God has no beginning and no end, but we do, and He is patient enough to wait for us to understand His will. Now that we know who He truly is, we can say with certainty that there is nothing outside of Him. He IS love, and His Word is true, faithful, and good.

May this be the beginning of a life in full with our Lord.

Close with a prayer for your students, thanking God for all He has prepared for us and for the hope it brings us, and ask the Lord to guide your young people to remain strong in their faith.

Download the daily "Family" readings from www.e625.com/lessons.

NOTES

NOTES

NOTES

SOME QUESTIONS YOU MUST ANSWER:

WHO IS BEHIND THIS BOOK??

Specialties 625 is a team of pastors and servants from different countries, different denominations, belonging to churches of different sizes and styles, who love Christ and the new generations.

e625.com

WHAT IS E625.COM ABOUT?

Our passion is to help families and churches to find good materials and resources to aid in the discipleship of new generations, and that is why our website serves parents, pastors, teachers and leaders 365 days a year through **www.e625.com** with free resources.

zona de contenido
PREMIUM

WHAT IS THE PREMIUM SERVICE?

In addition to free reflections and short materials, we have a service that includes lessons, series, investigations, online books, and audiovisual resources to facilitate your tasks. Your church can access this with a monthly subscription to this service per congregation that allows all leaders of a local church to download materials to share as a team and make the necessary copies that they find relevant for the different activities of the congregation or their families.

CAN I TEAM UP WITH YOU?

It would be a privilege to help you, and our formal education possibilities exist with that objective in mind. Visit **www.e625.com/Eventos** to find out about our seminars and events, and enter **www.institutoE625.com** to learn about the online courses offered by the E 6.25 Institute.

DO YOU WANT UPDATES?

Register now for the updates of **e625.com** depending on your work environment: Children- Pre-adolescents- Adolescents- Youth.

LET'S LEARN TOGETHER!

Magazine
Books
Chat
Downloads
Subscription
Store
Events
Seminars
INSTITUTO
e6
25
Online Education
www.InstitutoE625.com
e625.com